This book is for Chris — I'm
glad I met you!

Cover photograph by Lyndon
Johnson – that's his name – honest!
Camera borrowed from Nikki

Contents

PREFACE

Having lived on the Costa del Sol for a few months, I couldn't believe some of the things I saw and heard. Nothing specific, it was just whacky listening to some people. After a year you think you have seen it all and heard it all, but there we go again, some more twaddle. You never stop being surprised by some of the scams which go on and some of the complete crap you listen to from Brits living on the Costa del Sol, and Spaniards!

'Never take people at face value.' That's a true statement wherever you live, but down here you couldn't do that even if you were prepared to. If you did, then it would inevitably be expensive, very expensive indeed. Talk about skeletons in the cupboard; some people living over here have a full graveyard.

'Many very rich people move to Spain and go home rich' – read that again!

Many not so rich people move over here from the U.K. and go home absolutely and utterly skint, potless. They move to Spain, leave their brains on the plane, jump straight in with both feet and don't think things through. They trust people they shouldn't trust and lose the lot. It is very sad, but unfortunately it is not unusual.

The number of times I said to Chris, you could write a book about this lot. I said it so many times that I did write a book, and here it is. I want to stress that this is not a guide book; it is an account of my own experiences and my observation of others. It is a light hearted, lay man's view of life on the Costa del Sol.

There are so many man traps you can fall into over here, and so many frustrations. Trying to get anything done is a mammoth task; it's like walking through treacle. All too often Brits get it completely wrong and their dream life turns into a complete nightmare. It's so easily done, believe me.

The main reason that British people fail when they move to the Spain is the old 'fools rush in' syndrome. The best advice I could offer to anyone who is considering moving down here is to come over first of all for a long extended holiday. The longer the better, in order to look, listen and learn. There is a lot to learn. If you come with the 'I know everything' attitude, then you will inevitably get bombed from a great height. There is someone on every street corner waiting to take your money away from you, and many succeed. I am not proud to say that many of these people are Brits. There isn't the legal protection which is taken for granted in the UK, and scruples do not exist.

I am certainly not an academic but I like to think that I am a fairly quick learner, and I am a good observer. Covered in this book are a number of topics which are drawn from my own experiences. I have made mistakes, everyone makes mistakes. If by writing this book I can save other people from making the same mistakes, then I will have achieved something. I wish the information in this book had been available to me prior to moving to Spain. I would, without a doubt, have saved a fortune!

INTRODUCTION

Faster, faster, like a hamster in its wheel, running just to stand still. It's the norm' isn't it, in the UK? That's how I saw myself for the last few years of my working life in England. A hamster in a wheel!

My partner Christine and I had a very good life style. We lived in a large detached house with a huge garden up a private drive near to the moors above Halifax. We took at least two good holidays a year and had two new cars on the drive. We could eat out more or less whenever and wherever we chose. Life was good. We worked hard for it though, very hard indeed.

Life couldn't be much better could it – of course it

could!

Chris and I moved to southern Spain in September 2001. Prior to our move to the Costa del Sol we had more often than not taken our holidays on the smaller Greek islands. We usually chose the ones which you could not fly to direct as the fewer people we saw on holiday the better. Not that we were anti-social by any means, but two weeks of doing absolutely nothing was paradise to us. We enjoy each others company.

As well as the two week holidays on a Greek island twice a year, Chris often went to Fuengirola for the weekend or for a few days more. Her children, Jonathan and Justine, had lived on the Costa del Sol for a number of years. Jonathan had moved there first and got into selling time shares. Justine followed some time later as seeing her brother living in the sun appealed to her, as it would to most teenagers. I occasionally joined Chris but my work did not allow this very often. Fuengirola was never a place we particularly took to for a holiday as there are too many people and it is too commercialised for our liking. Never mind, if you have the sun on your back, does it really matter where you are?

I was the sales director of a large, Leeds based printed packaging company. Chris ran the accounts department at a road haulage company on the outskirts of Bradford.

I had been based in Leeds for about eighteen years. A couple of the later years in Leeds were spent flying all over the place on business. At that time I did a lot of business in Saudi Arabia and Morocco, with trips to Egypt and North Yemen thrown in from time to time. Combined with these trips was the fact that my company was, at that time, on the acquisition trail. As such, I was also spending time at newly acquired companies we had purchased in the U.K., France and Holland. I would go into my local pub on a Friday evening and friends would say to me, 'where have you been jetting away to this week then Stuart?' Paris, Amsterdam, Cairo, wherever. 'Oh you lucky bugger, what a life you have,' they would say. It sounds great, and to start with it is, but after a while you get absolutely sick of spending hours in airports and eating in hotels. It's also quite lonely most of the time. I could fly to Paris and back in the day. Yes, I had been to Paris, but I hadn't actually seen anything apart from an airport, the inside of a taxi and the office I was visiting. It's not as great as it may seem.

After that, the three years prior to moving to Spain were spent commuting from near Halifax to Hinckley in Leicestershire. That was a round trip of two hundred and forty miles. My company had made a major acquisition in the form of our biggest competitor. This company had a turnover well in excess of twenty million pounds per annum and was haemorrhaging huge amounts of money every month. The group board of directors brought in directors from different disciplines within the existing group with a view to analyzing the business, restructuring it, and turning it around. I was asked to be the sales director for what would be, probably, around three months. I really enjoyed this challenge and the people at Hinckley were great. Parts of the business were moved to other sites within the group and other parts of the group were moved in. My three month stint turned into three years as I was asked if I would take the job on a permanent basis. The directors, managers and staff worked very hard indeed on what was an incredibly difficult task. There were also casualties of course. Up and down the motorway most days to the point where I swear I knew every sign post and lamp post on that stretch of the M1. During our first full financial year we made a very small profit (pennies), but this was one hell of an achievement considering the huge losses when we took the business over.

Those three years were complete hell in terms of travelling and the amount of time I was away from home. Chris was very supportive, but she wasn't at all happy with a situation which began as a three month temporary position and turned into three years. After the first two years we considered moving to Leicestershire and looked at various properties in and around Market Bosworth. Fortunately we didn't buy. Around that time a major retailer who were very important to our company were making loud noises about moving large chunks of their printed packaging business overseas. It didn't feel right, so I suggested to Chris that we put the proposed relocation on ice for a while. Sure enough the business was taken away from us and the writing was on the wall that the company would not survive. The lost business in question was not only significant in size, but was very profitable. Without it we would be shafted and as the fixed overheads of our factory were huge, even major surgery on the head count wouldn't work.

There's Bob Hope and there's No Hope—we were shafted!

Every avenue was explored, from a sale, to breaking it up, to downsizing. None of the numbers stacked up so the decision was taken to close the plant and every employee would have to go. That was around two hundred and fifty people, good people. What a waste! Three directors, including myself and the commercial manager were retained for a further three months in order to pull as much cash back as possible through chasing debt, selling stock, raw materials and machinery. You name it and we tried to flog it. We were on an 'earn out' bonus and it was an opportunity to generate good money. As I had been with the company for over twenty years in total, and a director for twelve years, the money they would have to pay me was significant. I could have stayed with the company and gone back to Leeds but towards the end, having been offered jobs on similar or more money, my mind started to wander.

One evening after my usual trip up the M1 I pulled up our drive, stopped, slid down in the soft leather seats of my new Saab and closed my eyes. I remember it well, it was like a vision – 'bollocks to this, I just don't want to do it any more!" Let's move to the sun and enjoy life. Why not, we are only here once as far as we know. I'm not aware of anyone coming back to tell us otherwise anyway. I started to think about the fat pay slip which I had in my pocket for that month. About half of it went to other people including the chancellor.

Gross pay   x

Net pay   y   aaaaaaargh!

Who the hell has got all that then. We all more or less know the answer to that one and don't like the answer – do we? I can't ever recall seeing the chancellor on the M1 at 5.30 a.m. in the morning. I could do 1,500 miles a week, no problem. I could get home at 8.30 p.m., eat a lovely meal which Chris had prepared for me, a quick gin and tonic if I'm lucky, and then fall asleep. I just sat there in the car, thinking, for about twenty minutes. I then went inside our house and shared my thoughts with Chris over a gin and tonic or ten. I didn't know how to raise the subject. My initial thoughts were that she would consider me to have gone completely insane. Give all this up, why? Chris and I are great mates and her reaction was something along the lines of, 'well it's a huge step but let's talk it through and consider it.' We sat down night after night and discussed the best way forward.

We decided to do it, let's go for it!

We would sell our house and move to the sun. As long as we protected our capital, if it didn't work out, then we would just return to the UK and jump back onto the old hamster wheel again. It was exciting, it was an adventure, a dream. I remember one evening joking to Chris and saying that I felt like a pioneer. That one comment made me sit bolt upright. I remembered something that my old boss, Hugh Donaldson once said to me –

Shit, I said, the pioneers are usually the ones who return with arrows in their back!

Let's think this one through thoroughly, it's going to be a massive step. Chris and I had to do absolutely everything in our power in order to ensure that our dream didn't turn into a horror film.

First of all we had to decide where the hell to go. Moving away to live on one of our beloved Greek islands, that would be the ultimate wouldn't it? Well actually, probably not. Tourists see these tiny Greek islands whilst on holiday in the summer and they are paradise. In the winter however, many of the local inhabitants either go to Athens to drive a taxi or disappear into the hills and mountains to pick olives. Many of the picture postcard coastal villages are virtually deserted during the winter and there is no airport. Let's just say you got something like appendicitis in December, you would probably die. Seriously!

Going on holiday to the sun and moving permanently to the sun require completely different considerations and priorities. We would have to consider infrastructure, medical facilities, winter climate, banks and much more. As Chris's children were already on the Costa del Sol that was the logical move to make. We considered just about everywhere you can think of but when we listed all the things we wanted, common sense told us that the Costa del Sol was the place to go.

Decision made!

CHAPTER ONE

Off we go then!

What about our dog? We couldn't leave him; he was part of the family now. We got our dog from the battered dog's home at Adel near Leeds. It was a typical children's scam. My son Oliver, who was around ten years old at that time said, 'yes Dad, of course I will take him out for regular walks and really look after him,' yeah right! We named him Dino. If it was good enough for Fred Flintstone, then it was good enough for us. When we chose him he was the one sat at the back of his cage cowering whilst the other dogs were jumping up and down barking and generally going mental. Dino had apparently been in the hands of drug addicts on the Seacroft estate near Leeds. The poor thing had cigarette burns on his nose and all down his left front leg. To this day, I cannot even begin to understand how a human being can treat a dumb animal in this way. It makes you wonder who is actually the animal. The dog's home reckoned he was eleven months old which seemed rather specific at the time, but who were we to argue. He was a typical five bob mongrel, black with a white chest but he had such a wonderful temperament. We paid around a tenner for Dino and when we collected him we immediately went to the pet shop and spent around a hundred pounds on a basket, bowls, and all the other things you need when you own a dog.

Job done – in fact, as it worked out, it was 'jobby done!'

I had taken delivery of a very nice, brand new BMW three weeks prior to this episode in our lives. When we were about two miles away from our house with a lovely badly done to dog on the back seat with Oliver, Dino dumped all over the place. I'm driving, when all of a sudden all hell broke loose. Oliver and Chris were shouting, 'stop – the dogs crapped all over the back seat,' and this strong smell permeating throughout the car. Emergency stop, grind to a halt, banging my head on the steering wheel in complete panic. What the hell have we done? I know what he's done, and I don't want it. How on earth can I take customers out in a shit machine, let alone drive it a couple of hundred miles myself tomorrow. Get home as soon as possible, forgive him, I will grow to love him, honest! I don't like a dirty car on the outside, but when it looks like a student's toilet on the inside and

I'm the silly bastard who is going to have to clean it whilst probably being sick myself then – oh – what can I say.

Needless to say, Oliver took Dino out for a walk about twice, ever!

Chris began sorting out the dog ready for his new life abroad. Injections, an electronic in-plant chip and all the other preparations for his dog passport. Can't be bad can it, from the battered dogs home near Leeds, to retirement on the Costa del Sol. They say it's a dog's life, I don't think so.

Once our important decision had been taken, everything moved into gear quickly, too quickly really. Our house went on the market and sold within a few days which put the fear of god into us. We then sold some, but not much of our furniture. We had already taken the decision not to jump straight into the Spanish property market. We would rent for at least a year and ideally get something unfurnished as we wanted our own furniture around us. Having had a good life style in the UK we didn't want to rent a furnished property and feel like we had gone back to a teenage bed sit lifestyle. From what I had seen of some of the furnished properties, they were like a set from 'The Young Ones.' You get what you pay for, but having our own furniture around us was a must.

We then proceeded to sell off all the other things which would be surplus to requirement. There was a large garden water feature, a petrol lawn mower, a multi-gym 'hardly used,' carpets, and many more things. From our house being sold we gave ourselves around five weeks to get everything organized. This wasn't really long enough.

The people who bought our house wanted to move in almost immediately which didn't suit us, but rather than risk losing the sale, we agreed. A removal company came, packed everything up, and took it into storage until we called it over to their depot in Fuengirola. Where were we going to live for four or five weeks? It was impossible to rent a house or flat for such a short period of time and it would cost an absolute fortune to live in a hotel. Fortunately a guy called Phil McGuire who we knew from our local pub, had recently bought a very large old pub in Sowerby Bridge. He had the whole place converted into very high quality 'yuppy' flats. They were all glass, chrome, polished floors and stainless steel, very nice. Phil rented these apartments out for long term lets but as we knew him, he kindly let us have one for four weeks right up to our day of departure. Thanks again Phil, we still owe you one.

Meanwhile my company car went back which I was very sad to see go. One more piece in the jigsaw was missing. I had been a scooter boy in my teens and had owned during those years a couple of beautiful, fully chromed up Lambretta's. Ever since then I had yearned for a Harley Davidson motorbike. It's a blokey thing I guess, but when you are younger you can't afford something like that. When you can afford one, you are in grave danger of looking like some sad old git trying to relive his teens. I had already broached the subject with Chris and as usual she was great. 'You've earned it, go and get one' – yippee! I went down to the Harley dealership in Leeds as excited as a school boy going for his first bike. By sheer fluke they had on display a brand new Sportster Custom 1200 in one of the colours I had chosen. My heart raced and I almost ran to the bike in case someone bought it before me. Considering the time factor available to me, I wasn't in a position to place a factory order for a specific colour and I was more than happy that they had this one in their showroom in pearlescent blue and silver. I immediately said that I would have it, so I sat down with this guy to complete the relevant paperwork. I remember it was a Monday and he said I could collect the bike on the Friday. I'm sorry I said, but you will have to deliver it to my house near Halifax. 'Deliver it, why?' Er, because I can't drive a motorbike! I am sure you can imagine that some of the people who work in Harley Davidson dealerships are often huge, hairy arsed hells angel type people. This guy just stared at me and it was written all over his face, 'you f------- tosser!' It's true, I couldn't drive a motorbike. In my teens I had passed the motorcycle test on one of my scooters. As such, I would have been perfectly legal and entitled to drive that 1,200 cc Harley straight out of the showroom. If I had done, I would probably have killed myself and half the population of Leeds. I didn't even know how to operate the foot change gears. Seeing the fat Building Society cheque in his mitts, the gentleman concerned agreed to deliver the Harley to my house on the Friday as requested. There was logic in what I was doing. I immediately booked a one to one course with a motorcycle driving instructor. It cost me, but he brought me up to road standards in no time. I then arranged for the removal company to return and collect my new prized possession. The bike was shipped with the furniture.

Rather than fly to our new life in the sun we decided, mainly due to Dino, that we were going to drive. We would drive to Plymouth, catch the ferry to Santander, and then drive through Spain. My car had already gone, but we had bought Chris a brand new Ford Ka only a few months prior to our decision to 'clock off.' We would drive the Ford Ka over with the dog on board. The Ka was certainly not ideal as obviously the steering wheel was on the wrong side. Also, Chris never liked the aircon' in my cars and always chose hers with a sun roof and no aircon.' In the Spanish climate we would need aircon' but it would have to do. We would drive it to Spain and then just run it until it dropped. The car was only around six months old so we would lose a fortune if we sold it with no part exchange allowance. As it happened, two weeks before we were due to sail, I was driving past our local VW/Audi dealership just outside Halifax. Sat there on the forecourt was a one year old, new shape VW Beetle 2.0i. If you remember when they first launched this car onto the UK market, you could only buy left hand drive, and there it was. It must be fate, it has our name on it, and it was meant to be. Well, not quite. The car was in a baby sick sort of lime green. Still, you can't have everything so I veered into the garage, did a deal on a swap for the Ford Ka, and away we go. Drive to Spain in a left hand drive car, albeit looking like a hairdresser in a daft looking Beetle.

On the day of departure, we first of all took Dino to the vets for his final check up and his dog passport. We then drove to Plymouth via Bath. I loved the City of Bath and Chris had never been there so we took the opportunity of spending an evening and a morning taking in the sights. I had previously booked us into a hotel which accepted dogs, so we were sorted. We arrived in Bath late afternoon, had a wander around, a meal in a nice restaurant, and a few beers. Well, quite a lot actually. Next morning we had another wander around and then jumped into the car and off to Plymouth. Here again, I had booked us into a dog friendly hotel but we had to take an early night as the ferry left at 9.00 a.m. in the morning for the twenty four hour crossing. We had booked a cabin for the trip as we did not relish the thought of trying to sleep on one of those aircraft type seats with screaming kids running around amongst all the pissed up lunatics. I know you do get pissed up lunatics on ferries as I seem to remember being one of them once on a trip to the Belgium beer festival. Oh yes, and on the way back again! For the duration of the crossing Dino had to stay in the car. When we booked the ferry we were told that dog owners could go to their car every three hours and walk their dogs for ten minutes. I assumed, wrongly, that a crew member would accompany dogs and their owners around the deck. It transpired that what actually happened was that a crew member would unlock the door to your particular car deck and you could walk your dog around that. If you have ever been on a car ferry, you will know that the cars are packed in so tightly that you have to virtually limbo dance through and around the cars. On top of all that, the floors on some decks are not solid; they are similar to the top deck of a road car transporter. That's right, think about it. The floor has holes in it and when your dog goes to the toilet; the chances are that whatever comes out drops onto the deck below. More than likely onto the roof of a car or worse still, onto a roof rack full of luggage. Very nice! Next time you take a cabriolet onto a sea ferry – look up! All credit to Dino, he held himself in the car between toilet breaks but every time I went down to walk him I had visions of one hell of a mess on the lime green and yellow seats. We were lucky, very lucky indeed. We saw cars with large dogs in them and some had more than one dog. There must be a significant number of very unfortunate people whose cars look like a muck spreader has travelled through them by the time the twenty four hour crossing is finished.

Once in Santander we were off. I drove none stop to Fuengirola apart from petrol and short toilet stops for Dino. The Beetle was loaded up to bursting point plus the dog and every time we stopped and opened a door half the stuff fell out. I swear we must have looked like the Clampets out of the Beverly Hill Billy's. A proper couple of gypo's in a daft car.

So, here we are in southern Spain – yippee – I think?

Did we know anything – no!

We were at the beginning of an incredible journey. The miles we had travelled meant nothing. The journey had only just begun, as the real journey was the learning and we had not even sat in on one lesson yet.

Are you a quick learner?

CHAPTER TWO

Is life handsome or ugly on the Costa del Sol – it can be both!

When we arrived we had our accommodation sorted out for the first three weeks. A month before we made the epic journey to Fuengirola, Chris had flown out in order to find us a rented property for three weeks which we would use as a beach head. We figured that we should be able to find a more permanent unfurnished property within those three weeks, so we paid through the nose for a town house at holiday let prices. The house was in El Cotto, just outside Fuengirola. It was in the, what I would call, 'just okay' bracket. When Chris came over to find the place she could only view the property from the outside as it was allegedly occupied at the time. It did look nice from the outside but the inside did not do justice to it. Don't get me wrong it was clean, but the furniture was well past its sell by date. There was also a permanent lavatorial smell on the ground floor which we never got to the bottom of – so to speak! We expected better, but it was too late and the agent already had our dosh. We just put it down to our first bad experience.

Chris and I immediately began looking for a more permanent rented home and were guided by Justine and Jonathan. We didn't know the good areas from the bad areas, but we knew that we didn't want to live in the middle of town. We had three weeks to find somewhere suitable or it would be into a hotel for us. The local English speaking newspaper, the SUR in English, comes out on a Friday and we worked our way through the property rental section and dropped on a villa which sounded interesting. This villa was on the road up to the village of Mijas so we phoned the agent for a viewing. It was just what we were looking for, two bedrooms, two bathrooms, private gardens with palm trees and a private pool. The property was furnished, and just like the town house the furniture was crap. Through the agent we asked the owner if he would take the furniture out and he agreed. The pay back was that his furniture would have to go into our garage which meant that my beloved Harley would only have a car port. It was a compromise I didn't like but as the villa was very nice, we went for it and signed an eleven month rental agreement at 1,400 euros per month – sorted! They say that paying rent is a waste of money but to Chris and I it was money well spent. We know for an absolute fact that if we had bought immediately, then we would have bought wrong. We settled into our new home and called our own furniture in from the removal company depot, together with my Harley. We quickly found our way around and during the first few months made various acquaintances. That was an experience in itself, believe me.

The Costa del Sol is a magnet for the British and there are some great Brits living here but believe me, never in my life have I experienced such a tight concentration of full weight idiots. You could make a hobby out of sitting in British bars and just listening to the absolute twaddle coming out of some people's mouths. I am not talking about tourists, but Brits who actually live here. You have the 'yea right millionaire' who looks anything but, and is anything but a millionaire. Don't get me wrong, there are lots of genuine British millionaires on the Costa del Sol and you can get a flavour of this by just looking at some of the houses. There are however, lots of two penny millionaires who sit in pubs pissed as arse holes and spouting forth complete bollocks about how rich they are. There are the cowboy builders who also sit there as pissed as arse holes at 2 o'clock in the afternoon telling you how busy they are, which of course is why they are sat there at 2 o'clock in the afternoon.

There is the bar owner who is falling off his buffet telling you all about HIS bar and how busy it is – 'come down sometime for a drink – hick – it's great – hick – you will enjoy it – hick – must go now – hick,' – oh shit, he's fallen over! Honest – you sit there wondering if it's (National Talking Bollocks Day), and if it is, then why hasn't it been advertised.

Many of the Brits living in the major resorts on the Costa are hiding from something or someone. It's either the tax man, the police, the bank, a credit company, the CSA, or in a few cases all of them. We have met and heard of numerous people who cannot or dare not go back for the reasons mentioned above. It is not unusual due to the ease of credit in the UK, for Brits to build up the confidence of a bank and then take out a loan for £10,000, £20,000 or more. They then jump the country for a new life in Spain. Others build up huge debt on credit cards, Amex, Barclaycard, you name it. They go to the limit and then leg it to the nearest airport. They then proceed to get everything wrong and burn the money in a relatively short period of time. Due to the difficulties of finding a (proper job), which I will go into in more detail later, they are then seriously up the shit creek without a paddle. They can't afford to live in Spain and yet they dare not go back to criminal charges in the UK.

We became acquainted with one woman who had done just that. Fortunately for her, she had a son in the UK who had made a reasonable amount of money in a business. As a last resort she asked him for financial help. Being the loving son he was, he agreed to lend (give) her £10,000 – very nice! Unfortunately for her, presumably due to the fact that her son wasn't aware of his mother doing a runner with the bank loan, the son transferred the money straight into his mothers UK account. The Bank in question was the same one that she had taken the loan out with and surprise surprise – whoooosh – the bank said 'thank you very much,' and kept the ten grand. Believe it or not this lady was absolutely playing hell and spitting blood all around Fuengirola. She was saying how unfair it was that the bank had kept HER money. She really believed they had acted in an unfair manner and that the money was hers by right. Needless to say, the last thing she wanted the bank to know was her whereabouts, so that was that. Thanks a lot son, back to trying to find a job in a bar I guess.

WE HAD A BAR – Well, not quite a bar.

When we arrived in southern Spain we knew that we were going to take at least a year out to look, listen and learn. We knew that ultimately we would have to generate an income as we did not have enough capital to just sit on our hands forever. Chris had always quite fancied an English Tea Shop. Often when returning from visiting her children she would comment that there were hundreds of bars and restaurants, but nowhere had she seen where you could sit and have a nice cup of English tea served in a proper little ceramic teapot, and also get a nicely presented sandwich.

After a few months easing in, we started to casually look around at potential sites for our tea shop. What an eye opener that was. As a tourist you cannot look behind the curtains into the kitchen but if you are looking at bars and restaurants with a view to buying them, then you obviously see the lot. It shouldn't be allowed. Never in my life did I begin to imagine how absolutely filthy some of these places could be. If you can imagine the biggest shit hole student kitchen then you can double the filth and you still would not be anywhere near. On many occasions we just got to the kitchen door and turned on our heels, we wouldn't even go in. How do they get away with it – Christ knows. We were shown one bar in Torreblanca (East Fuengirola) and when we arrived the middle aged couple who owned the lease were absolutely legless. This was eleven o'clock in the morning and I kid you not they were completely and utterly off their trolleys. I have since learnt that this is not particularly unusual.

Chris and I completely agreed that if we were to live and work in Spain, then one thing was absolutely not negotiable, we have to be overlooking the sea. We didn't have any pre-conceived ideas on where to site our tea shop but highlighted two probable locations due to the volume of potential customers – Fuengirola and Benalmadena. Mijas Pueblo (village) was a possibility at one stage as we were living in a rented villa close to Mijas and loved the Spanish village atmosphere. After a short while we dismissed the idea of Mijas due to the lack of tourists in the winter and lack of a sea view. You can see the sea from certain places in Mijas, but it is around three miles away!

Whilst looking at potential businesses we were also sussing out menus and pricing. Presumably because there are more bars and restaurants in Benalmadena, the prices there are generally cheaper. We didn't like that. What's the point in working harder and for more hours for the same amount of money?

Fuengirola it had to be then!

We looked at more bar and restaurant units than I care to remember and to be honest, we got absolutely sick of looking. We put the idea on the back burner and concentrated on our other potential business venture in advertising. The idea was quite simple, advertising on beer mats. In the UK this is big business and a number of people have made a lot of money out of it. Traditionally beer mats were used to advertise beers, spirits and tobacco brands. When tobacco advertising began to be frowned upon and eventually banned, certain individuals began to ask themselves; why not advertise other products on beer mats in pubs and restaurants? The brand is spread all over tables and in your face. A great idea!

As previously stated, I had been a director of a print group and one of these companies printed beer mats. I had not been in Spain very long before I noticed that beer mats were rarely on display in bars. When I asked a few bar owners about this, they told me that beer mats were like rocking horse shit and hardly ever supplied by the Spanish brewers. If the beer representative did bring in mats, then it would inevitably be one little pack of around a hundred mats which many bars can go through in a day. That's it then. I have the contacts for the design and printing of the mats, all I need are the advertisers. We formed an official SL company which is the equivalent of a limited company in the UK. We then bought one million mats from the UK to our own design advertising the concept to potential advertisers. We had English on one side, Spanish on the other side. We then proceeded to blanket bomb bars along the whole Costa del Sol with our mats. I sat next to the telephone waiting for the response which I was confident would be almost immediate. It wasn't. I have learnt the hard way that what is successful in the UK does not necessarily carry through over here. We did receive calls from relatively small British owned companies over here, but when I told them the price they nearly fell off their chairs. They couldn't afford it or were not prepared to afford it. I had meetings with various companies and in some cases it was, 'I cannot afford to pay all the money at once but I will pay some now and the balance later.' Now, I have been around the block a few times. It is bad enough being striped when you work for a company but being striped for your own money is very painful I would imagine. No thanks. I thought the major real estate companies over here would jump at this new concept, but I was surprised and disappointed in their view that beer mats were 'not really in keeping with their image.' That's a laugh. What do they think their image is? Possibly they should do some market research on that one!

In the UK most campaigns are generated and driven through advertising agencies. Chris and I decided to hire an interpreter and spend some time in Seville where the major ad agencies are for this area. We secured appointments with numerous agencies and here again; disappointment was the order of the day. Drip mats are part of the UK culture. There are not many pubs you go into where there are no beer mats advertising anything from airlines to recruitment agencies. I quickly realized that the Spanish are not really tuned into the concept. When you start a meeting with the question 'what's a beer mat?' it is not a good start, you are on the back foot straight away. When I explained the concept to these people through my interpreter I then got comments back such as, 'but when I put my glass on it, I cannot see the advertising.'

Never under estimate the difference in cultures!

The only way to kick this off now was to try and generate business from UK companies who may be interested in advertising their brand or product to holiday makers and ex pats on the Costa del Sol. I secured an order from The Sun newspaper 'News International,' and the campaign went well. During the world cup every table in many sports bars along the coast had mats advertising the newspaper in bold bright red. I was delighted, but the elation was short lived. I spent an absolute fortune on telephone calls to the UK speaking to literally hundreds of advertising managers, brand managers and marketing managers. I drew blank after blank. I still had contacts at large companies who own Global and pan European brands. Some liked the idea but it was too niche for a major brand. One such company told me that if I could cover the whole of Spain then they would be interested in pursuing it but the Costa del Sol alone was too niche. There was no way I could even consider doing this. Where's the resource, where's the dosh! Distributing beer mats all over Spain would be a complete none starter for me, think of the logistics. Even if I was prepared to go for it then where would I be, back to long hours and hassle. On the old hamster wheel again I guess, running round and round – no thanks! Remember, what works in the UK does not necessarily work in Spain and often for reasons you would normally not consider. That initial experience in advertising cost Chris and I in the region of twenty thousand pounds. Not a fortune to a company, but to individuals (us) it hurts! Our business still exists and ticks over, but I believe UK companies are missing a trick here. Visit our web site and have a look – www.mediamatcostasol.com

There are many free newspapers for Brits on the Costa del Sol but the one which everyone wants to read if they are looking to purchase a property or business is the

SUR in English. I was reading the businesses for sale section out of sheer boredom one week and there was a small advertisement for a bar on the Paseo Maritimo (Promenade) in Fuengirola. We hadn't looked at any for a while so we decided to phone the number and view. When we arrived we couldn't believe it, exactly what we were looking for. It was a coffee bar/cafe with a nice sized, clean, well equipped kitchen, immaculately decorated and very clean throughout. You could walk in and start the next day – perfect. To make things even better, although the lease wasn't cheap, the rent was a steal for the sea front (I will explain the different lease costs and rents later). Apparently the rent was cheap because the occupiers prior to the people we bought it from were running it as a kebab shop and left it in one hell of a state. The freehold owner agreed to the low rent providing the new owners completely gutted the place and made something decent out of it. I have to say they did an excellent job. We didn't have to think about it for long as this kind of business, in this location, and at this level of rent, just didn't come up very often.

As the good book says – 'He who dithers gets f---k all' – we bought the lease!

The one thing this unit did not have was air conditioning and we had seen the previous owners in action for a day just prior to taking the keys. This was in July and sweat was literally dripping from her nose whilst she was cooking. I got a UK owned air conditioning company to install two large units, one in the bar area and one in the kitchen. This, in my opinion, is the best money you will spend if you decide to buy a café, bar or restaurant over here, particularly if you intend cooking. Once we signed the necessary papers and handed the money over we were given the keys. Although the unit was immaculate, there were things we needed to do in order to turn it into 'our tea shop.' First of all we changed the name as to me the name is absolutely paramount in putting over the right image and message. You have to tell people in the name just what you do. Are you a coffee shop, a restaurant, a pub – what? We called ours The Tea Tree; it has a nice ring to it. The next job was to scour Malaga looking for individual ceramic tea pots for one person and little matching milk jugs, cups and saucers. We spoke to virtually every food and drinks supplier in the area in order to hopefully source the best goods at the right price. We must have done a reasonable job there as we retained the same suppliers throughout, except one. This guy brought us in a box of frozen Cajun Chicken pieces and we noticed the 'best before' date had expired four months earlier. Excuse me; this chicken is out of date. 'Oh that's no problem, I eat it all the time and it doesn't do me any harm.' On your bike pal, you won't be supplying here any more. Stock rotation, QC checks – none!

Next door to us was an evening bar and as we had no intention of working evenings we struck up an agreement with the owner. We would use his terrace during the day and he could use ours during the evenings, a sort of time share terrace. A win win agreement. This doubled our outside capacity and worked well for both of us.

Chris and I didn't have a clue how many people it would take to run the business but rather than get swamped and sink, we would take someone on to run the terrace. As it happened a girl had been in a few days previously asking for work and had left her telephone number. We gave her a call and she explained that she had actually found a job but that her best friend, who was over here with her, was still looking. Fine. We arranged to meet her and she was a terrific girl. Her name was Emma and she was from the Isle of Man. Emma and her friend were over for the summer season so that's it, sorted, let's get cracking, three of us—utterly clueless! Emma had no terrace experience as she had worked for a Building Society on the Isle of Man. Chris and I didn't have a clue either. It was mid August and the first few days were horrific as we had not anticipated how busy we would be. We had already dramatically changed the menu as the previous owners menu was far too complicated, keep it simple. Most of our business, apart from the obvious teas and coffees, were toasted sandwiches and freshly filled baguettes. We didn't want to do breakfasts but considered we had to as 'The English Breakfast' is what many, if not most Brits want in the morning whilst on holiday. The original inherited menu had three breakfast choices. There was a small breakfast, a standard breakfast, and then what was called a 'mega breakfast' which was a full heart attack on a plate. Sack that, we did the standard breakfast and that was it.

You would not believe the trouble a breakfast can cause as you always get people who try it on and want something for nothing. The sausages and bacon are by far the most expensive components of a breakfast but we would regularly get people asking–

'I don't like tomatoes; can I have an extra sausage instead?'–NO!

'The breakfast comes with two eggs, I only want one egg. Can I have an extra piece of bacon instead?'–NO!

To begin with our breakfast price included a tea or coffee and we would get couples in saying something like, 'one breakfast please. My wife doesn't want anything as she will have the free tea I get with my breakfast.' Oh, that's alright then!

Within a couple of weeks the menus were changed again with the tea and coffee charged separate. Having done that, we still had not completely solved the problem. With the breakfast came a small complimentary orange juice–'Instead of the orange juice could I have a coffee?'–NO!

One couple came in and the man asked for a breakfast–fine. The woman then said, 'you see this two slices of toast with jam and butter, could I swap the jam portion for bacon?'–NO. How the hell can you compare a small jam portion with bacon? I wouldn't lower myself, what are they on. We even had a cheeky bastard who asked if he could swap the complimentary orange juice for a strawberry milk shake! It wouldn't be so bad if they had a wry smile on their face when they asked, but in most cases, they look at you as if you are being completely unreasonable when you refuse.

This is a strange thing which I never really got to the bottom of. If you were asking for two breakfasts, what would you say? Personally, I would say, 'two breakfasts please.' I reckon nearly fifty percent of our customers said, 'two breakfastses please.' I don't think the plural of breakfast is breafastses, is it? If so, when you ask for six breakfasts, do you say 'six breakfastseseseseses please? It's a strange thing that.

We pressed on through the first few weeks and Emma turned out to be an absolute brick. She was brilliant with the customers and as she only worked part time (10.00 a.m. – 2.00 p.m.), she would be there within minutes of us phoning her if we got battered. Emma stayed on the terrace taking orders and clearing the tables. Chris and I would alternate in the kitchen with one of us in the middle doing the drinks and the till. When things got stressful which was almost always at the beginning, an order would be ready in the kitchen and Emma would be chatting to a customer or taking an order. It was common to hear a hell of a loud shout coming from inside – 'Emmmmmmmmmmaaaaaaaaa' – the poor girl would colour up and fly in to collect the order. Chris and

I would feel terrible that we were shouting at Emma but she just got on with doing a superb job. I apologized to her one day and tried to explain that it was all new to us and that we were getting too stressed out. She just turned round in her kind mild manner and said, 'its okay Stuart, I understand, you can bollock me if you want, I don't mind.' We never shouted again as we felt a right couple of nasty gits. Unfortunately Emma's friend decided she wanted to go back home and one person on bar wages could not generate enough money to pay for an apartment and living costs. Reluctantly Emma went back too, but we still keep in touch with her and remain good friends. In fact, during the relatively short time we knew her, she almost became a daughter to us. A great girl!

In our previous working lives, Chris and I had never worked directly with the public and we were about to get one hell of a shock. We had already taken the decision to open only six or seven hours a day and settled on 9.30 a.m. to 3.30 p.m. Many of the bar owners over here open at 10.00 a.m. – ish and then don't finish until daft o'clock the next morning – no thank you! During the winter months we worked six days a week closing on Sundays. During the busy summer months we closed an extra day a week on Saturdays also. Now this seemed logical to us but really confused other people, particularly other bar and restaurant owners as their view was to work as many hours as humanly possible during the summer in order to make hay while the sun shines. Not us, if we hit the number we required in order to cover all our costs then that was it. In the summer we could do that and more in five days so we closed the extra day. If we went through a period of taking a battering every day, then we would sometimes take a spur of the moment day off. We called this a (St. Fuck Its Day) and I have to say that he is by far my favorite patron saint.

During the whole time we had our business I could not put my hand on my heart and say which days we were busiest. The only predictable thing about owning a bar or café is the unpredictability. One week we would be bombed out on a Tuesday and quiet on the Friday. The following week it could be exactly the opposite. The same applied to mornings and afternoons. No pattern whatsoever, which usually made it impossible to bring in extra staff at certain times or on specific days.

We were fortunate in the fact that we didn't need to generate much money and we were determined to enjoy our new life rather than exchange it for a new hamster wheel in the sun. We had not come to Spain to get rich; it was the lifestyle which attracted us. If we could cover all our costs for both the business and home then we would be happy. It was hard work during the summer months but we were looking at the sea all day, wonderful. I often thought to myself, 'this is okay, I used to make decisions on buying £1,000,000 + printing presses and now all I worry about is if we are going to run out of lettuce.'

Chris and I met some really tremendous people. We

also met a number of full weight knob jockeys. Any of you who have ever worked in a shop, pub, restaurant, or with the public in general will know what I mean. We were not prepared for some of the things that happened. To give you a flavour of some of the things we had to put up with, we have listed a few examples below. These are Gods honest truth – enjoy them, I didn't at the time –

Do you live here?
No we commute from Leeds/Bradford Airport every morning, what do you think?

Do you sell monkey tea?
Pardon.
You know, monkey tea, do you sell it?
I'm sorry; I don't know what you're talking about.
Monkey tea, I can't remember its proper name, monkey tea, do you sell it?
The penny dropped, she meant PG Tips – silly cow.

Will it be hot tomorrow?
How the f– - k do I know.

How long have you lived in Spain?
Four years.
Do you like it?
No it's crap you silly sod, what do you think?

A coffee please.
Certainly, black or white.
Brown please.
Eh – what's that, is it me?

Do you speak English?
Me thinking I'm having a laugh – Well Yorkshire, it's similar.
Oh that's a shame; I really wanted someone who speaks English.
What's wrong with everybody – can you believe that?

A scone with cream and jam please. How many servings do you get in a scone?
Are you having a laugh?

I think I would like toast and marmalade. Could I have a look at a piece of your toast please?
What?

A BLT please but with no bacon, tomato or mayo'
That's just an 'L' then; she wants a f----g lettuce sandwich!

(For this one you need to imagine a slack looking girl with a very strong south Yorkshire accent)
Av yer got spo-i-dick? She meant spotted dick which in the north of England is a pudding.

47

No sorry. We have apple pie, scones, cheesecake and chocolate fudge cake.

Aw, I wan – ed spo-i-dick really. Aven't ya got any spo-i-dick?

No sorry.

Aw – amt yer got any spo-i-dick at all?

NO NO NO – but by the look of your boy friend he can probably help you out.

One day a rather large lady came in with an older couple who, I think, were her parents.

Older lady – A prawn salad baguette please.

Man – A tuna salad baguette please.

Large lady – A prawn salad baguette please if they are big – oh and a cheese and ham toasty, and I think I will have cheesecake and cream please. I don't know why I'm ordering so much, it must be my nerves.

Your nerves, yea right. It's nothing to do with the fact that you're a fat greedy bastard then?

Then there are the stereotypes –

People who don't take sugar – what's wrong with them?
It's happened literally hundreds of times. I take a cup of coffee or tea out to a table with the standard issue spoon and paper tube of sugar on the saucer. The (none sugar taker) then proceeds to lift the paper sugar tube by the corner to face height, pulling a pained face as though the

48

tube was radio active and says, 'you can take this back, I don't take sugar.' So fucking what! Why can't they just leave it on the saucer until they have finished their drink, does it offend them or something? It's as though they want the whole world to know that they don't take sugar, who cares.

The Brit who has learnt a bit of Spanish. The Tea Tree was a typically English name, we had a full size Union Jack flying outside, and I have asked them what they would like in English –

'Dos café con leche por favor.'

Yea, right – that's two coffees with milk then eh!

The Thieves. You would not believe the things that people will steal whilst on holiday. We regularly had stolen toilet rolls, air fresheners from the toilets, serviettes, someone once stole a teapot lid – why not the whole pot for Christ's sake. People would ask for extra sugar or butter portions sometimes. Chris and I would often watch them out of the corner of our eye; it used to have us in stitches. When they thought nobody was looking they would pick up the sugar sachets and slide them into their pocket or bag. On a couple of occasions, just out of devilment, I would shout out, 'ey, I saw you nicking that sugar,' and then watch them colour up and look around them acutely embarrassed. You've got to have a laugh!

The cosmopolitan jet set Spaniards – These guys would come in occasionally and this would usually be if we had a couple of good looking British girls sat on the terrace.

They would sit there laughing and generally trying to impress the ladies. We had a couple of flash boys in once and sure enough they sat next to a couple of blonde girls on our terrace. I walked up to them and asked what they would like –

'Two Martini's on the rocks but with no ice please!' – You cocked that one up lads!

'666' – Damian 'the anti-Christ kid' – There are shed loads of them. What a little git. No please, no thank you, not even a kiss my arse. Are the parents on another planet? 'Don't do that Damian, oh please behave, would you like a Coke love' – bribery – it doesn't work! I don't consider that I was brought up the hard way, but if I had done a fraction of what Damian does then I would have got a right good crack around the back of the head, and deserved it. You could shave his head and find (666) underneath, he's not normal – is he – no, surely not. I have had said to me on numerous occasions 'you don't like children,' not true. I just don't like badly behaved children who have no manners. People sometimes say, 'It's not the children's fault, it's the parents.' That maybe true, but it still doesn't endear you to the little plonker!

What will the next generation bring to the world? A lot I hope. They couldn't make a bigger mess of it than our generation did. Could they?

The penny pinching tight bastards – Well, I think we have seen it all here. You can watch them at the end table of the terrace, they sidle up when they think nobody is looking and stand there perusing the menu and whispering to each other. You can see them nodding up the road and saying things like 'a cup of tea is only a euro up there,' or 'its expensive here.' You can always get anything cheaper but what are you getting for your money. I liked to think that we were 'reassuringly expensive' and if you can't afford it then piss off – in the nicest possible way of course. We would watch people look at the prices and then wander off. Five or ten minutes later they would come wandering back, and just out of badness I got great pleasure in waiting until they had sat down and then said, sorry we have just closed. Gotcha!

We had a sign outside advertising take away baguettes for the beach or airport. People would come in for a take away, look at the menu on the bar, and say things like, 'is there a reduction in these prices if I don't eat in and take it away?'

No we charge more as you are getting it wrapped in tin foil and a plastic carrier bag – just piss off!

'I see you get salad garnish with the baguettes. As I am taking it away could I have chips instead of the salad garnish'?

No, you can piss off as well.

One danger sign is the person who comes in, looks at the menu, and then asks for something completely and utterly different than anything on the menu. It's a tea shop, a café, call it what you want, but it certainly is not either an a la carte restaurant or a bloody pick and mix shop. They are looking for the angle, save a few pennies, be a prat – not with me. We had lots of them. One example was a guy who came in and wanted two eggs well done, but not too well done, 'he thinks he is buying a steak,' two slices of bacon and two slices of toast. You may not believe it but I could tell, a complainer, a tight bastard, that was him, I knew it. Now I am not a chef but I can understand it when cooks and chefs tell me that one person like that when you are busy with a none standard order, can cock the flow of things up completely in a kitchen. At that time on our menu the breakfast was 4 euros 90 cents and consisted of 2 eggs, 2 bacon, 1 sausage, beans, tomatoes and a slice of toast. As Chris, quite understandably saw this as an oddball order we took the bill out at 5 euros and 15 cents. Sure enough we watched him look at the bill, pick up the menu, and then call one of us over. Right my friend I am ready for you. 'I have had two eggs, two bacon and two slices of toast and yet you have charged me more than a full breakfast which includes a sausage, beans, tomatoes and an orange juice.' That's right, <u>BUT</u> there are two ways of looking at this. As you will also see on the menu, two scrambled eggs on toast costs 3 euros 75 cents, if you then add the two slices of bacon at 70 cents each then you can see where we get the price from. 'But that's not the way I am looking at it, I know about these things, my father was a waiter many years ago.' I swear I just flipped. The guy was arguing about pennies and I don't need it. I said, I don't give two tin shits if your father was the Prime Minister, just leave what you want to pay and I suggest you go somewhere else in the future. I don't need your money. Just piss off – calm down Stuart!

There was a German couple, well, they might have been Austrian. I am quite good with accents so it was one or the other. The couple were probably mid sixties and sat down at the front of our terrace in the sun, the best seats in the house. I went out there. Hello, what can I get for you? The lady said 'get me a cappuccino.' I let those bad manners go as I like to think that I consider the differences in culture. I then turned to the guy and he said, 'nothing, I don't want anything.' Okay, so that's one cappuccino on a table for four at the front of the terrace in the sun. I must have been in a good mood as I just went inside and got the lady a cappuccino which I placed in front of her. I was half way back when I heard 'get me a plate,' eh – is she talking to me? Now I am getting seriously annoyed. Why, I said, 'because I don't want all this creamy froth on the top.' Why not order an ordinary coffee then, I said. Bite your lip Stuart. I went back in and brought the 'lady' a saucer. I then watched her scoop the froth onto her saucer and I just bit my tongue again. I looked outside a couple of minutes later and she had got a plastic bag from somewhere and began eating her own sandwiches out of it. Oh boy, that's it! I legged it out as it was now my life's ambition to kick these people out. Excuse me; you can't eat your own food in here. The husband then said, 'what?' You heard me; you can't eat your own food in here. 'Have you ever been to France,' he said. Well actually yes, I worked there for a while. 'Well it's quite normal to do this in France.' Eh! Now think this through, you have a German 'possibly Austrian,' talking to an Englishman, in Spain, about France – WHAT'S THAT GOT TO DO WITH THE PRICE OF FISH? I picked up the coffee cup, minus the froth, and told them just to get the hell out. He then has the nerve to say to me, 'you are a greedy man.' What are they all about, go away. I don't want you and I certainly don't need you. Am I in the wrong business? Yep!

The bar front bore – When we first opened, there were stools at the front of the bar for people to sit on. Big mistake! There is nothing worse than being busy and having some dollop stood in front of you talking about things in which you have no interest whatsoever. You look up and there he is – 'bell end Billy the bar front bore.' It's not a pub and I certainly ain't no landlord. Is there an art to being boring? It seems to me that some people can talk for ten or fifteen minutes and yet say absolutely nothing. Some don't even talk, they drone. Others try to tell you a joke and are about as funny as a dead bat! It only took about three days and the bar stools went into a skip.

The 'terrace hoggers' – There are people who just want a free sun bed. They will come in, usually in pairs, and order the cheapest drinks on the menu. They then get a book out each, probably on stamp collecting or something similar. They will always sit on a table which is directly in the sun and at the front of the terrace with the best view of the sea if possible. Ten minutes later they will at best have taken one sip from their drink. They will continually shuffle their chair around for the best position and you can tell that they intend staying there for the day. It's not a problem if you are quiet, but if you are busy and they can see that they are taking up a table for four unnecessarily, then wouldn't you think they would have the decency to drink up and clock off – no! I won't have it. I'm out there, excuse me but as you can see we are full and people are walking past because there are no seats, will you be long? In some cases they look slightly embarrassed, pay their bill and away they go. There are, however, the (I know my rights) merchants. 'I am paying for this drink and will take as long as I like over it.' Wrong answer with me pal as you are costing me money. No you are not paying for it as I am taking it off you – whoosh, it's gone. Let's now say that the drink was free, goodbye. Who needs their two euros?

Terrace Hoggers!

The man hating, left handed, vegetarian women – I'm okay, I'm a nice bloke, ask Chris. I've done nothing wrong to these ladies but they don't like me. I'm not a woman, so I cannot comment with any confidence about what they are thinking. All I know is that they don't like men, me, because I'm a man, that's all. What they have experienced with their previous men is their business but they just don't like me. Chris can go out to take their order and they are fine and friendly, but I go back out with the salt and pepper set and they lurch back as if I am going to smack them one and then give me a frosty look. What have I done? Nothing. They just don't like me for one reason only, because I'm a bloke. What have they got against blokes, we're not all bad, are we?

Sometimes you get it completely wrong – oops! – It is easy to misjudge people in this game. Sometimes you get it completely wrong and end up looking a full weight plonker like me. Sometimes people go through a stage in their lives when the only time they open their mouth is to put their foot in it – that's also me! On one occasion a woman wandered through from the terrace towards the toilets and I was just coming out of the kitchen having been in there for some time. Excuse me, can I help you? 'Are the toilets down here?' Yes they are but they are for customers only so I am afraid you will have to go somewhere else. 'But I have been sat on your terrace for half an hour, I am a customer. I have had something to eat and drink.' Oh Christ, I have been in the kitchen and she must have been round the corner where I couldn't see her. Cough, er, right, retire back into the kitchen. You prat!

One afternoon a couple came in and the female looked a bit butch and much younger than the guy. When I got to their table to take the order, I looked at the guy and realized he wasn't a guy at all. She actually looked more like a guy than a guy does, but it was definitely a woman. So what. Live and let live eh. They ordered their food, a couple of drinks and everything is fine. As it happened we were very quiet at the time, in fact they were the only people in. After a short while I noticed that Chris was talking to these two people and thought nothing of it when I wondered out onto the terrace to join them. Chris said to me, 'this man wants to know where the best place to change money is.' Shit – Chris, I tried to whisper, shut up please. 'What, he just wants to know where to go to get some money changed.' Very nervous, ha ha, er Chris, sorry to be rude but there is a problem in the kitchen, please come, it won't take a minute. 'Yes, but this man has paid and is going now. He wants to change some money.' I legged it to the kitchen, put my hands over my eyes and squatted on the floor. I don't know who I thought I was hiding from. Chris then came in quite annoyed and completely confused. She looked at me squatting on the floor and said, 'what the hell are you playing at, you embarrassed me out there.' I embarrassed you, for fucks sake Chris; they're a couple of dykes. 'Dykes, what are you on about? That man wants some help with directions, that's all.' That's the point my love, that man isn't a man, he's a woman, you know, a lesbian, a rug muncher! 'He can't be – – – – – can he – – – – – I mean her. Oh hell, I daren't go back out there now. Are you sure she isn't a man?' Fortunately these two ladies had done everyone a favour and left, otherwise we would have had to stay in the kitchen all day.

Due to accents, it is very easy to misunderstand

someone from another European country, even though they speak perfect English. One day a Dutch lady walked onto our terrace and asked me for a coffee and a cheese and ham toasty. A short while later when the lady had eaten her sandwich, her husband arrived. I was doing something at the time, so Chris walked out to take his order. When she returned she was mumbling something to herself and looked annoyed so I asked her what was wrong. 'What a tosser. Some Brits come over here and think they can get absolutely everything that they can get in the UK; we're in Spain for Christ's sake. He asked me for toast with lemon cheese, where in Spain can you get lemon cheese? I have told him we only have toast and marmalade.' A moment later the gentleman in question walked in looking confused and said to me in a Dutch accent, 'why can't I have toast with ham and cheese. You must have it as my wife has just eaten it.' I just cracked up. When he had said 'ham and cheese' the guttural type accent must have sounded to Chris like 'lemon cheese.' Got it wrong again!

The early morning alci.' It's a fact of life if you have a café or bar in Spain that occasionally you will have no sooner put the tables and chairs out in the morning, before he or she will be sat down before you saw them coming. The piss head! Unshaven, if it's a man, dirty and generally looking like shit. Sometimes they will have come straight from a night club, sometimes from a girl's apartment they have met the previous night, and sometimes they won't have a clue where the hell they have been. 'A pint of lager please,' or 'a brandy please.' We had them all to start with until I decided to tell anyone who looked the worse for wear first thing in the morning, 'sorry but our licence does not allow us to sell alcoholic drinks until mid day.' Most knew this was rubbish but what could they do about it so they just got up and staggered further along the promenade and into another place who would serve them. There was one Scottish guy who presumably lived locally. He would come in every now and again shortly after we opened. He was a smelly horrible looking person and he would sit there with his pint, bent over, looking at the paving stones and picking his nose. I don't want them. Would you go into a place if you saw some paraffin lamp sat there picking his nose?

One morning a young Geordie guy came in first thing and asked how much a coffee would cost. Not a good sign if someone doesn't know if they have the price of a coffee. To be fair he was a nice lad and it came out that he didn't know where he was staying. He was over with a friend for just three days. He had landed the previous day, dumped his case in the room and then gone straight to the bar as he was staying in an 'all inclusive hotel.' From what he could remember he had downed numerous pints of the local rocket fuel and then got a taxi with his friend to Bonanza Square in Benalmadena. They then proceeded to drink various loopy cocktails and got split up during the course of the evening. He not only didn't know the name of his hotel but he didn't even know which resort he was staying in. He had some blood on his shirt and I asked if he had been fighting. He couldn't remember but I suggested to him that by the look of it, he lost! As it happened Nikki and Lyndon, some friends of ours, came in shortly afterwards and they had lived here for a few years so knew a lot more about the geography of the place than we did. We sat down together and tried to get a few clues. 'If you got a tax to Bonanza Square in Benalmadena, can you remember how much it cost you and we can then narrow down the possible position of your hotel.' 'About ten euros, I think. It might have been twenty.' Oh Christ, what a state to get into. Not remembering the name of your hotel is bad enough, but not even knowing which resort you are staying in is serious (power drinking). There is only one all inclusive hotel in Fuengirola, the Gardenia Park, so I am afraid that was the only help we could offer him. He knew what time he was flying out of Malaga the next day so I suggested that as a last resort, he made his way to the airport and waited for his friend to arrive for the flight. 'I can't do that as I think (hope) that my passport is in the hotel room.' Off he trots to the Gardenia Park which is about a two mile walk away in a brand new pair of rubber flip flops which he had just bought as he had also managed to lose his shoes during the proceedings. I would love to know what happened to that guy. If he didn't strike lucky at the Gardenia Park then it would be a case of hiking to Benalmadena and then onto Torremolinos in flip flops – (Power Drinking)!

A couple of times a woman who was probably in her mid forties came in around 9.30 in the morning, drank a couple of beers and then left. She had a huge nose and a bright red face. Although she wasn't completely scruffy, she certainly wasn't straight out of French Connection's front window. She was usually pissed when she came in and didn't look a full shilling to me, which would shortly be confirmed. I decided that I didn't want her in, so if she reappeared, I would refuse to serve her. Sure enough, some time later she came round the corner first thing in the morning with a 'Kermit the Frog' glove puppet on her right hand. Oh no, surely not, can this be so. She was talking to this bloody thing as she entered our terrace and sat down. I was that gob smacked at first that I couldn't react at all. I just froze with my mouth open in complete disbelief. As I approached her, and before I could say anything, she asked me for a beer. Pardon, I said. 'A beer please.' Am I imagining this, is it really happening. A pissed up middle aged woman with Kermit stuck on the end of her arm trying to be a ventriloquist and wanting a beer. No, I said, I am not serving you. I am afraid you will have to leave. 'Kermit, this nasty man will not give me a drink. You ask him if you can have a drink then Kermit.' 'Could I have a beer please,' said Kermit. Like a daft prat I am now looking at Kermit instead of her. No, I am not serving you, I said to Kermit. 'Well, I want a beer Kermit, you want a beer, and this nasty man will not serve either of us. You have done nothing wrong Kermit, ask the man again.' 'PLEASE can I have a beer,' said Kermit again. I never intended this to be a negotiation but I'm sure as hell not going to stand there talking to a fucking frog, just get out, go away, please! She then started whispering into Kermit's ear so that I couldn't hear what she was saying. Eventually she got up and started wandering off with Kermit looking over her shoulder telling me what a nasty man I was. All the way across the terrace and for fifty metres down the road I could see Kermit bobbing around over her shoulder and nodding his head, probably still telling me what a nasty man I was. It ruins your day, you don't need it.

On the odd occasion that someone sat down and we hadn't realized they were pissed until it was too late, I would have the 'Ken Dodd' laugh with them. You should try doing this yourselves. I would get talking to someone who was the worse for wear and say to them, I bet you can't say this, – 'Ken Dodd's dad's dog's dead. Who killed Ken Dodd's dad's dog.' It's absolutely amazing, but nine times out of ten, if someone is pissed, they can say it perfectly. If they are sober then they stammer, stutter and spit all over the place and get nowhere near. Why is that?

The 'instant service' people. Wouldn't you think when people are on holiday that they would be relaxed? Not always. We had a woman who came in once with her son who I guess was about five years old. They sat down and for whatever reason she had a face like thunder; like a smacked arse. As usual I gave her a couple of minutes and then went out to take her order. She wafted me away and told me she was not ready yet. Ignorant cow. As it happened two couples came in together at that point and one of the men said to me 'we are starving, four breakfasts please.' I took this order straight to the kitchen and then went back out to the woman whose son was creating holy hell, screaming and throwing things around. She was still quite rude and asked for a proper mish-mash of things, a proper 'pick and mix.' Fair enough, I then took her order into the kitchen. A short while later the four breakfasts were ready so I took them out to the party of four. As I was walking past this woman she said to me, 'EXCUSE ME! I was here before these people and I haven't had my food yet.'

No problem madam, – whoooosh – I picked up her coffee cup together with Damian's coke glass and said, if you want instant service there is a McDonalds down the road and I suggest you go there. I then shouted through to the kitchen, Chris, cancel that order as this lady is just leaving. You don't need it. I don't have to put up with that crap from anyone, who do they think they are?

Tips area funny thing. If you go into a place and are happy with the food you are served, the level of attention and service you get, then it is normal to leave a tip. This is not obligatory but I think it is fair to say that most of us do it, particularly when abroad on our holidays. It's not expected and if someone comes into a place just for a drink then why should they leave a tip. However, if they have a meal and feel as though they have been made welcome then yes, a euro, ten percent of the bill value, whatever. The one thing which really pissed me off was when someone left one cent or five cents. I take that as a complete insult and would much prefer that someone just said 'thanks,' walked out and left nothing. One day a Scandinavian couple came in to our tea shop. They had a couple of drinks and something to eat then asked for their bill, all very pleasant. They also commented on how nice the food had been. I took the bill to their table; they paid, and then sat there for a couple of minutes before leaving. As they started to walk away I took an empty tray out in order to clear the table and there were three one cent coins on the table. Two pence, thanks a bunch. I must have been in a bad mood I guess, as I just picked up the three cent coins and chucked them along the pavement after this couple. They looked around in astonishment and the lady then proceeded to pick up all three of the tiny coins and put them into her pocket. Tight or what!

There was one fairly elderly couple who rented an apartment in the block above our tea shop. They came over for a month, two or three times a year. They hardly ever came into our place except for the odd coffee and to borrow things. They borrowed a vase once and kept it for a month! I can't put my finger on the reason why, but this woman really irritated me. When they arrived for one of their holidays the lady came in and told me that her uncle

Fred was very ill in England and as they did not have a telephone in their apartment, she had given her daughter our telephone number in case something happened. A bit cheeky I thought, but what could I do. For the next ten days or so this woman would religiously come in two or three times a day and ask if there were any messages. It began to really piss me off as they never bought anything. What is this a bloody messaging service? One day the phone rang when we were very busy and when I answered it the daughter explained who she was. She went to great lengths in order to tell me that her parents were very good customers of ours and could I give her mother a message. I then told her that her parents hardly, if ever, came in to our place except to ask if there were any messages. Anyway the message was that 'unfortunately Uncle Fred has passed away.' We were still very busy an hour or so later and were running around the terrace like lunatics when I saw this lady walking past. I must have been in a foul mood (again) and I am not proud of this, but I just lost it and ran to the front of the terrace and shouted, excuse me, it's your uncle Fred. 'Yes' she said, He's dead! – Oh shit, did I really say that? Off to hide in the kitchen again.

You actually learn, without realizing it, to be a ventriloquist. Silly bastard, ignorant git, I could do them all. It's something you don't consider when you decide to move into this kind of business, but in a short period of time you have to be all things to all men which isn't easy when you are busy. You have to be a waiter, cook, cleaner, tourist information, agony aunt, weather forecaster, entertainer, the lot. Then there were my occasional stints as the (Sales Prevention Officer!) It's difficult if you are in a bad mood and sometimes you take an instant dislike to people before they have even opened their mouths. Occasionally you find that they are actually very nice people, but more often than not you are spot on – ignorant!

When you have a bar or restaurant you have to put up with all kinds of things which you are not prepared for. Without going into too much detail, the lavatorial habits of some people are absolutely disgusting. I have to say that overall women are worse than men. When you serve food and the toilets are at the rear end 'excuse the pun' of the bar, it's no fun when someone disappears for more than a few minutes. You know instinctively that you have –

A DUMPER! It is something which Chris and I never got used to. Someone would disappear into the loo and then return more than a few minutes later. All you could do was wait. Sometimes we were pleasantly surprised. A lady may have taken so long as she was putting her lippy on, whatever. Many times however, the inevitable happened, one minute, two minutes, then, (the waft). Oh hell, they have turned the light off, and that turns the fan off. Quick, leg it to the toilet with the air freshener before someone else comes through –

If not, as they pass the bar the waft will hit them, and they might think it's me!

Allegedly by Spanish law you cannot refuse anyone a

glass of water or the use of the toilets. After only a couple of weeks of Spaniards and tourists coming in to use the loo, we had to take action. As it happened, there was construction work going on near us for well over a year so that was it. Chris or I would say, 'I'm ever so sorry but the construction workers have cut through the water supply and this will not be back on for approximately one hour.' Now our Spanish wasn't very good, so the Spaniards were more difficult, 'lo siento, construction aqui corto agua.' This was said whilst gesticulating ferociously as it was only half sense to a Spaniard. We must have looked like we were doing the birdie dance, but it worked. It's bad enough having a paying dumper!

People will steal almost anything that isn't nailed or screwed down. Shortly after opening, we had a Moroccan looking guy one day who came in for a glass of water. Next to the draught beer tap on the bar we had a small basket where we kept the tips. Paying customers would often throw a euro or whatever into the basket. Chris was in the kitchen and I turned my back for what must have been just a few seconds to fill a glass with water and then gave him the glass. He took a small sip and then left. Strange I thought, he only took a sip. About ten minutes later I noticed the tip basket had gone. The bastard, I gave him a glass of water and he nicked our tips. Not easy lifting a basket full of loose coins without making any noise whatsoever. Chris was seriously miffed about the (Tip Nicker). It was only probably ten or fifteen euros, but that wasn't the point. We had earned it and he'd nicked it. Chris kept going on and on about it and a few days later the ice man came in. Bars buy ice cubes in bags for ease and on this particular day the normal ice man must have been ill or something as it was a different guy. Now to picture this properly you need to understand that 'Ice' in Spanish is 'Hielo,' pronounced 'Yellow,' and instead of pronouncing 'Euro' as we do, the Spanish say 'Aero.' Okay, this different ice man comes to the door and shouts to us, 'Hielo?' I couldn't believe it, it's not like her. Chris started jumping up and down with steam coming out of her ears shouting at me, 'I'm sick of this, tell him to piss off, he's begging. He's asking for an Aero. He looks like that guy who stole our tips.' Calm down, I said, it's the ice man, he said 'Hielo' – you know – ice!' 'Oh, that's all right then – are you sure it's not him.' That ice man looked very sheepish every time he came in afterwards until the normal guy returned.

We never gave credit. I know so many bar owners who have been caught out big style by (the tab runners). These guys can drink. They start going into a bar on a regular basis, usually every night, and they will spend a fortune and pay as they go. The bar owner thinks all his birthdays have come at once as he has never taken so much money. After a few days, once the confidence factor has built up with the owner, they will start paying their bill at the end of the night. Then the inevitable happens and they start a tab, paying every second or third night. The final stage is that the tab builds up to a significant number and just like magic, these people disappear never to be seen again. We knew one lady bar owner who stupidly let this get completely out of hand. She was taken for tabs to the value of 1,200 euros. Do not give credit to anyone, ever!

Every bar and restaurant, or anywhere there are tourists in Spain, gets (the musicians). I use the term loosely as some of them would be better described as comedians. They are a bit like buses. Combined with the Lookie Lookie men who sell scam CD's, watches, hats and sunglasses, you won't see anyone for an hour and then you will get ten on your terrace within fifteen minutes. There is the singer with a guitar, the accordion player, you name it and somebody plays it, usually quite badly. There is one old guy who creases me. He arrives at the front of the terrace with something resembling a Fisher Price children's battery operated plastic piano. Just before he starts, you can see him flick a switch at the back and then pretend to press the keys. He gets quite carried away, exaggerating the key banging when it's obvious he isn't playing it at all. To make matters worse the tune is invariably Jingle Bells. Just what you want on your annual fortnight's holiday in the middle of August eh. He cannot understand why hardly anyone gives him any money, but nearly everyone falls about laughing at him. There is also a guy with a guitar who is a lovely friendly man but can't sing to save his life. He sings a song in Spanish, god knows what the words are, I think he made them up, but it is sung to that tune from the Cornetto advert. People give him money just to get rid of him. He scares the kids!

The Lookie Lookie men are as good as gold and really nice friendly guys. Most of them are from Senegal and I can say in all honesty that I have never seen any bother whatsoever with these guys. I have had a few watches off them myself and not had a bad one yet. Oh yes, apart from a Breitling which I noticed once the Lookie Lookie man had gone that it was spelt wrong, 'Brietling.' They haven't quite got the DVD's right yet. The guy will swear blind that the DVD you are purchasing is the one stated on the sleeve and yes, it is definitely in English, honest! You get it home and here we go again, it's in Spanish. Some are excellent but it is not unusual to get your DVD home, settle down with a cup of tea or a can of beer to enjoy your chosen film and turn it on. The picture is not too bad; yes it's in English, great. You will be watching the film and then all of a sudden some bloke will stand up and go to the bogs or for a packet of pop corn because it has actually been filmed in the cinema. Well that's great, my evenings well shafted again. You have to give the Lookie Lookie men ten out of ten for initiative though. They can be there on the sea front one minute selling watches, sunglasses and CD's, the heavens open and the rain comes down. Within minutes the same guy is back on the terrace selling umbrellas, it's fantastic, as if by magic. They must have hidden ammo' dumps dotted around the town for a quick change of merchandise. Occasionally the local police will have a clamp down on the Lookie Lookie men and confiscate CD's. As most bar and restaurant owners know, you would occasionally get one of them leg it into your bar, throw their brief case full of goods behind the counter, and saunter out whistling. You knew immediately that the police were around and he would be back in an hour or so for his case and away we go again. We went to the Sierra Nevada one day in March to see the ski resort. There they were, the Lookie Lookie men, selling designer bobble hats and ski gloves. Initiative, fantastic!

There is an Elvis impersonator in Fuengirola who appears to only work evenings. I have to say that he is quite good but he doesn't take any shit. When people come over to Spain for a holiday then they are not familiar with the currency immediately and it usually takes them a few days to get used to the value of certain coins and notes. Now Elvis doesn't appear to appreciate this as we have seen him on a few occasions finish his brief act at the front of a bar terrace and then walk round with a bowl collecting donations. He will look into the bowl and if someone has given just five or ten cents, he picks it up and chucks it back at the donator. Heavy stuff Elvis, calm down, you'll be having a heart attack – again!

Rarely a dull moment in this game. Every day is different, and it is different due to the public.

TEA SHOP PASTIMES

There were many times during the winter months when

we were very quiet for an hour or more. If it was a nice day then Chris would often take a little chair we had over to the beach and read her book in the sun. She would keep looking over and if customers came in then she was back in less than a minute. Perfect, what more could you want.

When you haven't lived in the UK for a while, you forget the stupid things that happen there. On the odd occasion that I bought an English newspaper, I would often have to read some of the articles twice just to make sure. Surely that can't be true. That's crazy. Is it April the first? Just for a laugh we would cut these stupid articles out (stupid but true), and put them on the table where we kept the magazines, tourist guides etc. We would have a hell of a laugh with the tourists who until they saw the cut outs had already read the article and thought nothing of it. This was because they were immune to some of the stupidity which goes on in the UK. A few which really cracked me up were in the 'you couldn't make it up' bracket.

'£250,000 a year to keep Diana's fountain open' –

I have obviously seriously edited the article due to the space involved, but the upshot of this article was that tax payers would have to fork out around £250,000 a year for the upkeep of Diana's fountain meaning **funds would have to be diverted from other services**. Due to people 'falling over' they have fenced off the fountain and will have (six) officers on site to stop people paddling. Allegedly the Culture Secretary said, 'there had been teething problems.'

We were asking customers if that meant the fountain was full of people's teeth who had fallen over.

'Shoplifters will not be given a criminal record' –

The upshot here was that a person would in future be given an eighty pound on the spot fine for shoplifting instead of it being considered to be a (proper) criminal offence. It said you can steal goods up to the value of £200. Right, so you walk into a shop and nick goods to the value of two hundred pounds and then walk out and get collared. You pay the eighty pound fine and you are a hundred and twenty quid better off. That's all right then!

'Bobby hide and seek' –

The worst crime rate in Europe apart from Sweden apparently. Where are the Bobbies. One day in a London suburb (seven) police people were seen hiding in shrubbery for an hour and a half trying to catch drivers doing illegal right turns at a T-junction. You're having a laugh – aren't you?

'No hard work please' –

A jobs consultant advertised for £5.42 an hour warehouse packers who must be 'hard working' – sounds fair enough. The local Jobs Centre banned the ad because it 'discriminated against people who didn't or couldn't work hard.' It cracks me up. I can see a company soon advertising for a lazy bastard who doesn't want to do anything but wants paying a fortune for the pleasure.

'Toothless Typhoon' –

This must be my favorite, it's so stupid. Now I don't

know much about jet fighter planes but, come on, this is not rocket science. Well I suppose it is really. The article stated that efforts to save money on the RAF's £20 billion Eurofighter Typhoon war plan, by scrapping its powerful cannon, have turned into a farce. Four years ago ministers announced that in order to cut costs the aircraft would be built without its wing-mounted gun. However, due to the jet's computerized flight controls, the cannon would have to be replaced by ballast the same weight and size otherwise it would be unbalanced. Engineers tried to make this replacement ballast from, wait for it, **concrete and lead!** This has got to be a wind up. Hang on, I'm wetting myself here – – – I'm okay now. It then dawned on them that the cheapest way to fit an object the same shape and weight as the cannon was to use – – – – the cannon! Well done guys. My five bob dog could have worked that one out.

I could go on, but needless to say we had some great laughs with these newspaper articles. The sad thing is that you can read a few, just as good as these, every day in the UK newspapers. What's wrong with the place?

I had a lap top in the tea shop and was connected to the internet. The computer was useful for doing our accounts, writing letters, booking flights, and generally keeping in touch with friends and ex colleagues in the UK by e-mail. I had never had so much spare time on my hands and liked to spend ten or fifteen minutes, whenever possible, e-mailing people. One day I received an e-mail from a good friend of mine called Steve Cartwright who had worked for me in the UK. Within the e-mail he told me that another mutual friend of ours had bought a small printing company near Shipley in West Yorkshire and he gave me the new e-mail address. Now this guy, who we will call David Smith, had always been easy to wind up and as we were not busy I decided to try my hand again. Below, in order, are the e-mails which went backwards and forwards over a period of two to three weeks. They are printed, quit literally, word for word. No exaggerations, word for word, apart from his name change as I would not want to embarrass him, honest! The spelling of the words is exactly as appeared on the e-mails – look out for Senor 'Kerr.'

Is he gullible or what?

Hola Senor Smith,

We are ad agency in Spain and av customers in Spain who will open soon in Shipley near you factory. He will require printed envelops, mail shots etc. We supply artworkings. Are you eentrested in this.

Regards,
Juan Alonso Jiminez

Hi
Very interested please contact me again with details.
Regards,
David Smith

Senor Smith,

As you are knowing the Bank of Spain tooke over Abbee Bank in Englettera. This must be confident but I tell you that in future printing will be bought from new officinas in Shipley by Publicidad Manager for all banks. Bank of Spain is my client.

Is this still interest of you.

Juan Alonso Jiminez

I am interested, what kind of print requirements do you have? Can you supply details?

Regards,

David Smith

Hola – I am the assistant of Senor Jiminez who is now out of the office for a day, possibly two. I am the person who will be holding meetings with potential suppliers both large and small as there is a large cross section of print and it will be our policy to use local printers wherever possible.

Although I am Spanish my father is Scottish so my English is fluent. What size of Company are you and is it large volume or small items of stationery you will be looking for. Do you print labels in reels and computer listing paper or do you have contacts locally.

Regards,

"Juan Kerr"

Please review my web site @www.!!!!!!!!!!!!!!!packaging. co.uk for details. I would like to hear from you regards all stationery requirements. Do you visit the UK? Or can I contact your agent? Please advise.

Regards,
David Smith
!!!!!!!! and Packaging

Senor Smith,

Sorry delay in reply. We have looked at website and your imprenta is good products. We now are furniture in officinas in Shipley and have local people to start working March. We will have talks sereos at your imprenta factory February.

For open new officinas and many employ we want to have Spanish fiesta and are doing a Bull Run thru Shipley wich is typical of Spain for Spanish Banco. You are local and hope you can help with me – we need 6 bambino bulls for 1 day and can you give telefonica number of farmer to get bulls from. We pay good money and will give you commissioner.

Gracias,
Juan Alonso Jiminez
Director

It went quiet for a while – then –

Dear All,
Please note my new e-mail address is !!!!!!!!!!!!!!!!!!!!!!!!!!!!!!!!
I would be grateful if you would update your records.
Regards,
David Smith

Senor Smith,
Gracias for yoor new e-mail. We are still working on print works for yoor interest. Have you any news for mee on bambino bulls yet. Men of Shipley are lucking forward to the bull run. Will you av a run and av you got insuransis een case ee catches yu.

Hasta luago,
Juan Kerr

That did it—he clicked—eventually! I won't tell you what he called me but what he still doesn't know is that half of the UK printed packaging salesmen were receiving copies.

Sorry—'DAVID.'

THE 'GRUA' TRUCK

Many an hour was spent watching the Grua truck. A Grua truck is basically, what you and I would call a breakdown truck. In Spain, if a car is illegally parked then the Grua truck will appear and just tow the vehicle away. They take no prisoners. If you park in the wrong place then your car will be gone when you return. What a performance to get it back. You have to go to the police station to pay a fine and then you have to go to the vehicle compound, pay another amount of money, and then get your car back. This can equate to around one hundred and twenty pounds. All along the sea front in Fuengirola are pay and display parking bays. As it happened, the bay directly outside our tea shop was for loading and unloading only i.e. Coca Cola, San Miguel deliveries etc. It was naughty because there was actually a parking ticket machine there, which understandably made many people assume that it was a legitimate pay and display parking area. There was a sign there informing you of the fact that it was for loading and unloading but this was placed directly behind a tree trunk so you couldn't see it. It is a cast iron fact that the grua truck, often directed by one or two policemen, would always pull away the hire cars and foreign plated cars first. The Spanish plated cars were almost always left, if not until last, then left there permanently. It's not fair, but it is a fact. Resident Brits would sometimes sit on our terrace and take bets on which car was pulled away first. It was easy money as if there was a hire car there, (you could spot these as they were inevitably fairly new cars with no wheel trims), or a foreign plated car, then it was gone first. You could bank on it. The Spanish look after their own you know!

THE LOCAL ALCI'S

Spain does have its own share of alci's. Another pastime

of ours when we were quiet was to watch the local alci's who congregated across the road on the beach. What a great set of guys. In the UK they would probably be abusive, but for some reason that's not the case over here. They would start to arrive at the same spot around 9.30 a.m. with a plasi' bag full of Cruz Campo beer cans and proceed to have their breakfast. Once the breakfast bag ran out there would be a constant procession from the beach to the local bakery for some more cans. 'Yes, the bakery sells beer.' As the day went on we would observe the laughter increase and then they would just go into a coma around mid afternoon, another good day. The one thing these guys did have in common with their British counterpart was the fact that they also had a dog with a piece of string around its neck. Why is it that tramps and alci's always have a dog with a piece of string around its neck? Although these guys were off their heads most of the time, they were very friendly and we got to know some of them quite well. If we had a problem they would always help us out, borrow a euro which you would never see again, and then fall over – until tomorrow!

Do you fancy a bar in Spain?

Let's move on.

CHAPTER THREE

Do you want a bar on the Costa?

It's easy isn't it? 'If I buy a bar, I can sit in the sun all day and everyone will want to come into my bar won't they' – NO!

There are so many horror stories with Brits who come over here. They jump straight in, don't understand how it works, have no business sense whatsoever, and go home skint after six months.

If you are considering buying a bar, café or restaurant in Spain, be aware of the options available to you. There are three main ways to purchase a bar on the Costa del Sol –

BUY AN EXISTING FREEHOLD

It depends how deep your pockets are. If money is not

an issue then buying the freehold on a successful existing bar is obviously the best investment. These are difficult to find and very expensive if they are any good as existing freehold owners do not generally want to sell them.

BUY THE FREEHOLD ON AN EMPTY UNIT

The second option is to buy an empty unit beneath a brand new apartment complex. These are also expensive and also fairly difficult to find as the Spanish tend to purchase these (off plan) units before building has even commenced. By doing this, they purchase at a much cheaper price than would be the case in a finished building. They will then sell the lease, usually to a Brit. The down side of purchasing or leasing a brand new unit is the fact that it is completely and utterly empty, a shell. You would then have to install all the electrics, tables, chairs, chillers, cookers, the lot. You are into serious money here and as such, most people go for the third option – leasing!

LEASING

No exaggerating, there are very few bars on the Costa del Sol which are not for sale at the right price (the lease that is). However, if you walk around any of the main tourist resorts you will hardly ever see a for sale sign outside a bar or restaurant. That is not the way it is usually done.

Whichever route you decide to take if you buy a business, make sure that you use an INDEPENDENT Gestoria and/or Solicitor. Agents and owners will tell you that in order to make things easier you should use their Gestoria and/or Solicitor. My advice would be to use a completely independent one. There is an immediate conflict of interest if you go with theirs. Ask around, look in the local newspapers, there are hundreds of perfectly good ones. If there is no attachment to the agent or owner then you will be given unbiased advice. That's the first step.

Never go with an associated person or company and under no circumstances sign anything unless you are 110% certain that your Gestoria/Solicitor has seen and understood the content of a contract or agreement. The 'go on, trust me' factor must be dismissed, no matter what. This may sound a bit cynical, but just assume that everyone is out to rob you and you can then be pleasantly surprised when you find they are not. You will be told that a bar has a music licence when it does not, it has a lifetime lease when in fact it has a five year lease, you name it. Get it confirmed, be sure!

Bars are usually sold through (agents) and as much as people hate the agents there are often good reasons why they are used by sellers. When a lease owner sells the lease, he has to pay the freehold owner between 10% and 30% of the selling price, depending on the agreement. 20% of the selling price is the norm' on transfer to the new lease owner. As often as not, what happens is that the lease owner will tell the freehold owner that they are selling the bar for considerably less than the actual price agreed.

Therefore paying out 20% of a lower figure. If the existing lease holder sticks a for sale sign outside the bar, then the freehold owner will probably send a friend pretending to be interested in buying the bar. He will enquire about the price – BINGO! The freehold owner then knows what you are actually selling it for and wants his full 20%. If, on the other hand, the leaseholder sells through an agent, then the freehold owner doesn't even know the bar is for sale. Instead of the actual (say) £50,000 sale, the leaseholder will declare he is selling the business for (say) £30,000. He has immediately saved 20% of the £20,000 difference 'four grand – thank you.' When the transaction is made, the £20,000 difference will be paid direct to the seller by the purchaser in the form of a briefcase full of cash. There is a trap that people fall into here. When a lease owner informs his freehold owner that he is selling the bar, the freehold owner has the right to say, 'well that's quite cheap, I am prepared to pay that for the lease and buy it back from you myself.' He has first option on it. If you tell him a price which is obviously too cheap, then he may call your bluff and buy it back himself at your deflated 'blag' price. You have lost out!

Like any walk of life there is good and bad. In the case of the (bar agents) over here, there are some real bad ones. They ooze insincerity! Some of them are unqualified, unimpressive, and in certain cases, completely incompetent. Some are failed ex bar owners themselves who have been previously striped by an agent, learnt the hard way, and probably thought to themselves 'what the hell, I've been done, I now know how I've been done, so I'll just go and do a few Brits myself.' Obviously not all are out of this mould and there are some very good agents (I think), but how do you know the good from the bad. At the end of the day most of them are only interested in their commission and they will quite happily sell you a complete and utter dog.

Unfortunately most potential bar purchasers leave their brains on the plane in Malaga. They haven't a clue what they are looking for and if they have not already contacted one or more bar agents through the internet prior to coming over, then they read the local rags and contact the agents.

It works like this. You buy the lease and the cost of a lease varies dramatically. Having bought the lease, you then pay a monthly rent for the life of your lease which is usually five years. At this moment in time (I take a standard bar or restaurant unit), the lease will cost you between £20,000 and £80,000 – yes that much difference. The cost of the lease can be looked upon as an investment as you hope that if you paid that much for it, then someone else will pay the same or more in the future when you sell. If it's a bad business, then there's always another clueless Brit getting off a plane.

Buying a bar or restaurant on the Costa is no different from buying a house or business in the UK in this respect – 'location, location, location.' But, put before that, the word – **RENT!** If that's not right, you are dead. Believe me you are dead, moribund, out for the count, skint, on a plane home. BEFORE YOU EVEN OPEN THE DOOR ON THE FIRST DAY – YOU ARE DEAD!

You can buy the lease for a bar in a backstreet for the lower £20,000 and you will probably die. It's Manchester with sun and as much as you might think that people will come into your place, the chances are they won't. If you go for the front line promenade then you will pay considerably more for the lease. It will be the top end of the price bracket plus more, depending on size and location. The lease will cost you more, but you are by definition going to get more passing trade. Holiday makers will always walk along the sea front as it's the done thing isn't it. The sea front does not guarantee success. It certainly helps, but look at how many other units there are in the immediate vicinity. Are they British, Dutch, Spanish? What are they doing and how busy are they? If there are a few units doing what you intend doing, then remember that you will only be diluting the business which is already there. Also, if there are other similar businesses, then the chances are that there will be a price war. There is always some idiot who wants to take what he or she thinks is the obvious solution. To stand any chance whatsoever you will have to be cleaner, better, and have more personality than the existing businesses.

Decide what you want to do before you start looking. Is it a bar you want, is it a café, is it a restaurant, do you prefer to work evenings or days. Too many Brits do not really know what they want to do. They look around and find a business they think they like and then carry on exactly as the previous owners did. In all likelihood, these people were not making enough money to make it pay, hence the sale to you. When you purchase a business you will not be looking at audited books, it doesn't work like that here. You will have (the word) of the owner and/or agent. Assume this to be a complete lie, because it probably is. Owners declare as little as possible and as such, any figures you look at will be made up. It isn't really all that important. Even if you were lucky enough to take over a business which did have accurate books (very unlikely), it isn't what the existing owner takes that matters. It's what you do with it. Remember there is very little good will here. If you bought a café or bar in the UK then you would inherit regular customers who would continue to use you if you maintained or exceeded the standards of the previous owners. In a Spanish holiday resort, you have very few regular all year round customers. By definition you are catering for holiday makers who will visit you a few times during their one or two week holiday and then disappear, probably never to be seen again. If you are really lucky then you will catch a couple or a family on their first or second day, they will like your products and your service, then hopefully come in every day. Even then, at best, you will only get a week or two out of them.

DON'T DO THIS!

In order to illustrate to you just how stupid some people are, listen to this. We came into contact with a couple from London who came over and wanted to buy a tourist bar. They were adamant that they would not use an agent as they had heard from someone in the UK that these agents slam a large commission fee on top of the owner's asking price. They would do the deal themselves as everyone has their price. This couple spent quite a few weeks doing what was in essence a pub crawl round Benalmadena, Fuengirola, Nirja, La Cala, Calahonda, you name it. They were looking, listening and generally doing all the right things as well as presumably getting off their heads most days in pursuit of their research. They narrowed it down and down until they finally decided they wanted to buy this particular bar in Fuengirola. I will never know why they chose this specific bar as although it is a very nice bar, it is not in a particularly good place for volume business. They began to regularly frequent this bar and got quite friendly with the lease owner. After a while this guy struck – 'I would like to buy your bar, how much would you sell it for?' The owner replied 'make me an offer.' '£75,000 the guy said.' Now I know that this bar owner paid £35,000 for the lease from someone who couldn't get out quick enough. He snapped this guys hand off, 'done, sold, thank you very much – knob head.' The rent on this place was 1,200 euros per month and nobody was going to make a good living out of it. Needless to say, this couple are now struggling like hell and wanting to sell as they are hemorrhaging money every week. The guy wanted this particular bar for whatever reason and was obviously determined to get it, but don't go straight in with a big offer. If he does manage to sell it now, he will probably have to take an amount there or thereabouts the original £35,000. He just lost forty grand, plus all the money he has lost running the place during his time of occupation.

Businesses sell for differing amounts of money and rents vary dramatically. In order to illustrate a typical scenario, I have generated a hypothetical situation –

SO, LET US TAKE (DAVE AND SUE AVERAGE) –

They sell their semi detached house in the UK, pay off their mortgage, settle up with everyone else (sometimes), and have say £50,000 in their pocket. A lot of money to most people.

They then get off the plane in Malaga and leave their brains on the plane!

Dave and Sue rent an apartment, room or whatever. Meanwhile they are being shown numerous bars by the agents. With fifty grand, you might think you are loaded but it soon goes if you are not earning. The agents will see Dave and Sue as a complete dream come true. They don't know the form, they don't know the geography, and they have little or no business sense. Hey – let's sell them their dream. If Dave and Sue arrive with £50,000, they will struggle badly to buy the lease on a decent bar and still have money to live on. They will inevitably finish up with a bar which is a complete no hoper for reasons which you would not even consider if you have just got off a plane from the UK. They will be shown what are called (starter bars). That's a laugh! They should call them suicide bars as whoever buys them, usually finishes up either completely skint and suicidal, or at the very least an alcoholic and divorced.

Let's try to be positive to start with. Dave and Sue are horrified by the price of bars on the sea front. They cannot afford this location so they buy the lease on a starter bar for say £30,000. That's more than half of their well earned money gone straight away. Once they get the keys they find the electrics are shot at, the chill cabinet doesn't work, the chairs are held together with string and there is a full council estate of cockroaches in residence. It's not what it appeared to be is it? 'Well, here we are. We will have to make the best of it and get these things fixed.' Another two grand at least! That's £32,000 out of our original £50,000 gone straight away.

The rub is the rent.

Strangely enough, the rent on a rubbish starter bar is often the same, and in some cases more, than the rent for a good bar. THIS IS ENGINEERED, IT'S DONE ON PURPOSE!

Let's think this through. If you own the (freehold) on a bar or restaurant and it is in a position where you know it has not, does not, and will not ever be a good business, then you can sell the lease quite cheaply. There is always someone who cannot afford the going rate for a good one. You then charge a high rent. It is unbelievable that many people think it is great to get a bar for a cheap price (the lease cost that is), but they don't think through the rent. If you have a high rent in a bad location business then you are chasing stars, big numbers, all day, all week, all month.

Having left their brains and common sense on the plane, many people don't even consider it, but you can easily generate a rough business plan for a bar or restaurant on the back of a cigarette packet or a beer mat – does it stack up financially or not?

These would be typical costs for an average Starter Bar, with a cheap lease.

Cost of lease: Say £30,000 (45,000 Euros) cash outlay – 'park that for the moment'

OVERHEADS PER (WEEK) IN EUROS – based on 28 working days per month

The Bar –

Rent	250
Electricity/Gas	60
Gesoria (accountant)	31
Terrace Tax	32*
Bar insurance	14
National Insurance '2 people'	110

IVA on rent (VAT to us)	35**
Company/Personal tax	30
Repairs and renewals	20***
Refuse/bins	2
Pest control	6

590

* You must accrue for your terrace tax. If you have an outside terrace then you will be hit with a significant bill once a year. In Fuengirola, this is presently payable in May so if you buy a business early in the year then the bill will hit you quickly. Terrace tax varies depending on the square metres (area of your terrace), and as an example ours was 1,800 euros per annum. A big hit if you are not expecting it!

I cannot comment about other Spanish towns but here again, in Fuengirola, if you can prove that you live in the town itself then you get a 30% reduction on Terrace Tax which is well worth having.

** You should also accrue for this item. The freehold owner has to pay IVA (VAT) on the rent he collects which at present is 16%. In reality he collects this from YOU and you need to be aware of it as it is yet another cost to your business.

*** Allow for repairs and renewals as you will always have a chiller requiring a new motor or thermostat, a microwave packing in, something will happen. We had to get new scissor gates on the front of our unit which cost 1,000 euros. If you are not accruing for repairs and renewals then this is a big whack to anyone.

You also have to live of course

Home –

Apartment rent	200 (800 euros per month gets you a decent furnished 2 bed apartment on an 11 month contract)
Apartment electricity and water	15
Petrol	20
Car insurance—say	12
Mobile	30
Shopping	120
	────
	397
Total	**987**

That's near enough 1,000 euros per week you need to take, just to stand still – BUT – don't forget about your stock. You have to buy stock in order to sell it. Work on around 30% of your turnover going to pay for the stock you sell. This will depend on what you sell i.e. drinks only, drinks and snacks etc. etc.

So that takes it, in round figures, to 1,300 euros per week you require just to stand still.

No going out for a drink, the odd meal, buying clothes, shoes – 'holidays' – you need to add some more on for that so add it on. You are fooling yourselves if you don't!

How much do you think you will spend on these items?

Don't forget also, that if you do take a holiday – that's a (double whammi). Not only do you have to accrue for the cost of the holiday, but you also lose the takings for the duration of your holiday. You are not working for someone else now you know! It also assumes that a couple are going to run the business completely alone with no paid help or staff. Can you manage that?

One last point – your opening licence will cost you, in round figures, one thousand euros so allow for it!

Okay – let's now see how many punters we need to generate the necessary revenue –

You can pitch the (average spend) where you like but do not under estimate the number of people you will get in who will only buy one drink, a beer, a coffee, a soft drink. You can increase the 3 euro average spend if you want, but don't kid yourself – it's your shout!

Turnover

A) Assume 50 customers per day each spending an average of (say) 3 euros

=150 euros per day

That gives you 900 euros per week based on working 6 days

B) Assume 100 customers per day each spending an

average of (say) 3 euros

= 300 euros per day

That gives you 1,800 euros per week based on working 6 days

Obviously turnover (A) is nowhere near enough. Turnover (B) is not a bad little business. Not good, but not bad.

The fact is that if you are behind the front line on a back street where there are inevitably other competing bars, you haven't a cat in hells chance of getting 100 customers in per day. Don't kid yourself. Forget it. You are bust!

How many hours a day do you want to work?

What about the winter months?

We know of so called starter bars in Fuengirola and Benalmadena which are lucky to get eight or ten people in a day. In the winter they may not get any. So many people buy a bar without doing simple sums and then cannot understand why they are losing money hand over fist. Many do not have deep pockets. When they fall behind with the rent they try to sell on the lease. If they can't sell quickly they have no option but to put the keys back through the letterbox. The £30,000 or whatever they paid for the lease is gone. Their living expenses have also come out of the original £50,000 and they are on a plane back to the UK –

COMPLETELY POTLESS!

Freehold owner, 'thank you very much,' next please!

Only recently I knew a guy who sold the lease he had on a good bar and secured a very good price for it. With this money, he bought the freehold on a completely empty unit underneath an apartment block down a back street. The unit had been bricked up for years so he purchased the freehold for a song as the existing owner just wanted rid. This guy then proceeded to turn the unit into an extremely nice little bar. He knew where to go for fairly cheap furniture and also who to use for building the bar area, toilets etc. It looks nice, very nice, and he is now trying to sell the lease (during winter) for a very reasonable price. He has deliberately fixed the rent at a high level. To some innocent coming over here with a limited budget, it would appear to be a cheap lease price for a very nice, brand new bar. This innocent will be told that 'during the summer months these streets are heaving with tourists' and that it is an excellent starter bar. In reality there is no way the bar will take enough money to cover the high rent, running costs and living costs. Not a hope in hell.

(ENGINEERED) – Six months, nine months, it won't take long. The innocent off the plane will run out of money and give the keys back to this guy as he cannot afford the rent any more. Thank you very much – sell the lease in winter and away we go again – it's a cash cow. There is a hell of a good living to be made out of this if you don't have any problems sleeping at night.

If you are thinking of buying a bar or restaurant in Spain, do the sums. Sit across the road for a couple of hours per day at different times. Watch, not only the business in question but the street. How many people are passing, are they predominantly tourists, are there any busy bars in that street, if so what's so special about what they do. It is not unknown for sellers to rent a crowd for the visit of a potential buyer. If you look at a bar and it is full of customers then go back a few times. Don't fall for the oldest trick in the book.

Keep a reserve – Whatever happens, make sure that you have a slush fund stashed away somewhere for a rainy day (or ten). They will come, believe me. There are always things cropping up which you had not allowed for, as well as the bad weeks when you do not cover your costs. Not hundreds, you will need at least a few thousand as a back up because if you do not have it, then you are bust. There are more failures than successes and very few bars, cafes or restaurants see out the standard five year lease. They either sell the lease or go bust and hand back the keys.

It has to be done, 'a fag packet business plan.' Don't kid yourself, do it!

Of course not everyone plays by the rules. There are numerous bars and restaurants in Spain which are illegal. No opening licence, no music licence, owners and staff not paying National Insurance etc. etc. These are risks people sometimes take because they have no choice i.e. they are not taking enough money through the front door to pay for legalities, they can't afford them!

Let's assume that you buy a good little business. One

thing I would not recommend is cutting your audience. Many people do this without realizing it. Take a Yorkshire couple who want to call their bar The Yorkshire Boy. 'That will attract Yorkshire people like us won't it.' Well yes, possibly. It will also possibly put off any Lancastrian, Londoner, Scot or whatever from coming in. Then there is the Scottish couple. 'Let's call our bar The Scotsman.' The same applies. The name is extremely important and narrowing the audience is not a good idea.

The last thing I want to do is put people off from coming over to Spain and buying a bar, café or restaurant. However, it is important to have an insight into some of the traps you can fall into. I wish I had been able to learn something about (how it is) before we moved to Spain. We have met numerous people who bought businesses over here and succeeded but, to repeat myself, there are far more failures than successes.

One day we were working in our tea shop and a young couple came in. We were fairly quiet at the time and got talking. They were asking various questions about our business and then told me that they had just bought a bar. They were very excited about it. I asked them where and they told me. I instantly knew this place and my heart sank for them. Now this is a long row of bars which people refer to as (the garages) and (suicide row). They do resemble a long row of garages. I have never counted them, but I would say there are probably eighteen or maybe twenty bars doing more or less the same thing.

These units change hands at a frightening rate. They face over a car park apart from the centre five or six which look over rather untidy spare land. The wire fence for the spare land is about four metres from the front entrance to these bars so the view is, to say the least, not good. Also, in order to get to one of these middle bars, you have to walk through the neighbouring bars. Forget it; you're dead before you open. Who the hell is going to walk through other bars just to get to you unless it's your best mate. This couple went on to tell me that they had bought this (starter bar) through an agent. It was in the centre of the row – oh hell! Both the seller and the agent had told them that the spare land was to be landscaped by the council – honest! They also told them that once the landscaping was complete, the council would then give these bars a few metres of the new gardens to put tables on. 'That will make all the difference in the world won't it.' How nice! Never had I heard so much bollocks in my life. They were so excited and I didn't know whether to laugh or cry. These poor people had fallen for the lot and had just thrown their money down the drain. On the odd occasion I went past the garages, I would look over and see them sat on their own waiting for customers who didn't arrive. A few months later the bar was locked up – GONE.

A similar thing happened a while later when another couple started to come in on a regular basis. After a few conversations it came out that they had bought a starter bar and they would be getting the keys in a week or so. When they told me which street it was on round the back I thought – oh Christ no, you're dead. We actually got to know these people quite well, they were from Liverpool. Once they opened, Chris and I went round a couple of times for a drink in order to support them as they came into our place. There was never anyone in. They would sit there from 10.00 a.m. until midnight, every day. One week they took ten euros in the whole week and the writing was on the wall. It was actually quite a nice little bar but completely in the wrong place. Hardly anyone went down that street and if they did, they were invariably local Spanish people. The last thing they would do is go into a British bar where the prices are generally higher for the tourists. Three months at most, and they were shafted. Unfortunately this situation actually split them up as he went back to the UK. The lady, Brenda, stayed for a while and tried to get a job. Things didn't work out and she also had to go back to the UK. It's sad; Brenda is a lovely lady who just bought the wrong business.

Chris and I went for a drink early one evening and got talking to a father and son. They told us that they had bought a bar on the seafront in Torreblanca which is at the far eastern end of Fuengirola. They had only been in this bar for three weeks and were extremely disappointed at the number of people they were getting in. They were sure things would pick up shortly as there appeared to be a lot of people walking past going to and from the large hotel nearby. Oh dear! I did not have the heart to tell them as they had obviously not done their homework. That particular hotel is **all inclusive**. If they looked closer, they would see that most of the people walking past had little plastic wrist bands on. Why would these people go into his bar when they could stay in their hotel and get completely legless for free?

Another example, there are lots of them, is a guy who actually escaped disaster. He was a cockney who started coming into our place. He was asking all kinds of questions about running a bar/café and was anxious to buy one as soon as possible. Sure enough, a couple of days later, he came in all excited and told me that he had seen the perfect place, 'right on the sea front, lots of tables, yes, this is the one.' He explained to me which bar it was and as he had not yet paid a deposit I said to him, look, I won't advise you but if you don't mind I will point something out to you. 'Sure' he said, 'please do.' This bar you are so excited about, I know it. It is not the normal sea front type bar with a terrace directly outside the front door. It doesn't have a canopy over it with canvas sides which you can drop down in the rain or wind. All its tables are out on the actual pavement and there is no way you can put up a canopy. All you have are sun umbrellas over each individual table. 'Yes' he said, 'That's the one.' Well that's fine on the hot summer days, very nice, but what do you do when it rains or if it's a windy day. You know – winter. 'I don't know, I hadn't thought about that.' I'll tell you what you do – shut. You have no option. Who in their right mind is going to sit under a sun umbrella in the pissing rain or when it's windy? You are shut. There will be lots of days like that in the winter and you will have no income whatsoever. 'Oh, thanks for that.' He didn't buy that bar!

Think it through!

Some failures occur due to pure bad luck. Two gay guys took over a bar where Chris and I sometimes went for a drink after work. Now I have never mixed with gays or had gay friends and I was very apprehensive when I found out that these two were taking over. I had nothing against gays; it was just that they weren't in my world. Up to that point in time gays were just people who were called funny names in jokes like shirt lifters, clam diggers, fudge packers, up hill gardeners or whatever. It was a shock to me, these two guys were great! It just shows that ignorance is a dangerous pastime and I am genuinely ashamed of it. Pete and Gary became very good friends of ours, they still are. Anyway, these two guys cleaned, painted and generally did this bar up to the point where it was immaculate. They wanted a family bar and as such, encouraged anyone to come in and discouraged anything which would identify it as a (gay bar). They were gay, but they certainly did not want a gay bar. All was going well and they built up a good little business. Unfortunately, shortly after taking over, the council turned up one day and dug up the whole road outside their bar, pavements the lot. No warning, no compensation, nothing. The nice tree lined avenue at the front of their sun terrace became over night a holding area for huge concrete pipes and JCB's. That absolutely decimated their turnover for months and it is something you would never consider looking into prior to signing for a bar. Are there any serious road works about to begin? Fortunately they also had an entrance at the rear, 'so to speak,' so they managed to get through it but struggled badly. We still go into this bar to see our gay friends but Christ, have I had some stick over it. Back in the UK whilst based in Leeds, I had a sales force working for me and we were very successful. We also had a great laugh. As well as the business relationship we had, we were also very good mates and have remained so to this day. One of these guys, Shaun Chadwick, came over with his wife Sue and stayed with Chris and I for a few days. Sure enough, on a couple of occasions we took them to this bar and introduced them to Pete and Gary. Word got back very quickly. Two of the other guys who had worked for me, Steve and Adrian, now have their own printing business and within a few days they sent me an e-mail asking if I was taking it up the duck run – what on earth could they mean?

The price you sometimes have to pay for having gay friends – it's a small price, as they are great guys and I am proud to call them my friends!

Along the same road as our friends bar, there are two other British owned bars but these have only one entrance at the front. The roads were ripped up as were the pavements and it was an obstacle course just trying to enter these bars. Their turnover ground to a halt immediately and when they enquired as to how long this work would take they were told that storm drains were being installed and that it would take approximately six months – ish – honest! Now if you are chasing 1,100 euros per month rent, national insurance, all your other fixed costs, plus your own living expenses, then you need very deep pockets to see yourself through six months with virtually no turnover. What can you do about it – nothing. You either have the money in the bank in order to subsidise yourself for six months – ish, or you do not. If you do not, then you are bust and the money you invested in the lease (say £60,000) is lost forever. You may have been unfortunate enough to have bought the bar just prior to the road works. Your chances of selling it now when outside looks like a Dresden Street in 1945 are nil.

How deep are your pockets?

We knew a couple who bought a bar in a back street. They were convinced they would attract customers as the husband was a singer and entertainer. They opened up without looking into the legalities of having live music on the premises. Away they go, blaring live music out every night until daft o'clock and surprise, surprise, the neighbours were not happy at all. The police turned up one night, closed them down immediately, and padlocked their door. **'You need a music license for that you know'** – they lost the lot!

DO NOT SELL ON PRICE

This is a common mistake made by bar and café owners. They buy a bar or cafe, realize that it is not quite as easy as they first thought, and then wonder what they can do in order to improve things. If people are not coming in then what can we do in order to get them in. 'I know, I will be cheaper than all the others around me.' Unless you can purchase stock a lot cheaper than anyone else which you can't, then the only way anyone can make a half decent profit out of selling cheap is VOLUME.

The average bar and cafe in Spain is relatively small. If you have twenty people in, then you are quite busy. On that basis, volume is not going to happen. If you reduce your prices by say 20% then you require a considerable number of extra customers just to make the same money. Then there is the extra leg work on the terrace, washing up, cooking. The chances are that if you did reduce your prices by 20% you would not generate the extra customers in order to justify the price reduction. In other words, you would be working harder for less money.

Then there is (THE LOSS LEADER), what's all that about? A Café Bar just along the promenade from us started selling a pint of lager for one euro when the going rate was around two euros fifty. I was talking to the owner one day and asked him his train of thought on this one euro pint. 'Oh that's a loss leader. The one euro pint will pull them in and they will then order a meal or a sandwich.' Every time I walked past this place it was packed, but when I looked closely, I could see that everyone in there was drinking – yes, that's right – a pint of lager at one euro a chuck. Two weeks later the price was back up to the normal level.

Certain beer suppliers will give you a free barrel every fifth or sixth barrel purchased. Every now and again you will see a large sign outside a bar – 'Buy a pint and get the second pint free' – how stupid can you get. You get a free barrel from the brewery and you then give it away to holiday makers who you are not likely to ever see again. It is not as though there is good will and close customer relationships to consider here as would be the case with locals at a UK pub. Why give it away – SHED HEAD.

Actually if you are quiet, then there is a good argument for putting your prices <u>UP!</u>

Every now and again take a look at your prices. Ten cents here and twenty cents there on tea, coffee, a sandwich. Over a week it can make a difference and the chances are that you will not lose any customers because of it. As with any business, people will pay for quality and cleanliness. Rather than serving tea in a grubby mug with a tea bag floating on the top, use individual pots. Serve a sandwich with a small salad garnish. Make sure your toilets are always clean! People will gladly pay that little bit extra, and the chances are that they will come back the following day.

BUT WATCH THE DELIVERY MEN

They try it on! If you have a bar or café then during the course of most days you will receive a delivery of some kind or other. Its sods law that this delivery will arrive when you are busy and you will just point to where you want them to leave it, look at the price on the invoice, pay the guy as quickly as possible, and then get on with what you were doing. A little later when things have slowed down, you will check the invoice against the delivery and bang – a case of drinks short, a pack of cheese short, something. Watch these people, they try it on.

Running a bar in Spain, it's a laugh – honest!

CHAPTER FOUR

The Accountant

In the UK, people generally play by the rules. Okay people will bend them a little bit, but there is not a lot you can get away with if you work for a living.

In Spain, if you have a business then you have what is called a Gestoria, (you will have seen this name earlier in the book). This person is an accountant but he is also someone who sorts bureaucracy out for you, a sort of cross between an accountant and a solicitor. He can fast track documents which would take you as an individual forever to sort out, particularly if you do not speak Spanish. Gestorias do very well out of us Brits. Most speak perfect English as it is in their interest to do so. The Brits are good customers.

You have to live in Spain for quite a while before you realize just how much bureaucracy there is here. You go to one place to sort something out and are then sent somewhere else who directs you to another office. At each stage you will queue for eternity and the chances are that when you finally get near the front of the queue at the correct desk, at the correct office, then it will just be closing for Siesta.

Bureaucracy, red tape, queues – for almost everything.

Life is so different here and the rules are completely different. Sometimes there are no rules and if they do exist, then nobody quite knows what they are.

A guy we knew who had a bar long before we bought our tea shop was doing okay and asked his Gestoria one day, 'I have this friend (honest), who also has a bar and he was wondering whether he should give his Gestoria ALL his receipts at the end of each month or should he sort them out and throw a few in the bin?' The Gestoria smiled knowingly and replied, 'no, you should give me all the receipts and I will decide which ones to throw in the bin!'

The same guy wanted a mortgage for an apartment he had decided to buy. He asked his Gestoria about a mortgage so they sat down and discussed how much the property was, how much deposit he could pay, and how much he needed to borrow. Based on these figures the Gestoria said there would be no problem. The guy then asked, 'but this business doesn't make a profit on paper, how can you get me a mortgage based on the earnings from a bad business?' 'Oh don't worry about that,' the Gestoria said, 'I will pump your profit up for a couple of months and once the mortgage is issued I will take the profit back down again.' – Eh! Can you see an accountant in the UK doing that?

It is not that any particular Gestoria or Solicitor is bent, that is just the way it is. Any dodge is fair game and that is why there is so much so called 'black money' in Spain. Cash – Euro notes – lots of them. People are walking out of banks all the time with piles of cash in order to pay the (black) proportion of a purchase.

Another bar owner we knew, who had a completely different Gestoria, had a dilemma as his wife was going back to the UK for two weeks in order to visit the family. As they ran the bar together this meant that they either had to close, or bring someone in just for the two week period. Now this guy was quite unusual for down here as he played everything straight down the line, by the book. He wouldn't take any chances and absolutely everything was completely above board and legal. Rather than close the bar and lose the turnover, he decided to bring someone in for the two weeks. He spoke to his Gestoria and told him that he was bringing a lady in to help just for two weeks. How could he do this as he didn't want someone from the Town Hall walking in and asking to see this ladies employment contract. 'It has to be done properly.' His Gestoria turned to him and said, 'give me the name and

NIE number (National Insurance) of this person. What I will do is draw up a temporary employment contract for the two weeks. If someone walks in then her employment is perfectly legal. However, if nobody walks in, then give me a call after the two week period and I will just rip up the contract and it didn't exist.'

'Eh, er, okay. That's sorted then!'

Whatever you do in Spain, get a good Gestoria – it's vital!

That must be the shortest chapter in the history of writing. I wonder why it's so difficult to find much of interest to say about accountants?

CHAPTER FIVE

Apartments and houses – buying and renting

As mentioned near the beginning of this book, when people move to Spain they should be aware of completely different things to look and listen for when renting or buying property. You don't know the areas, just as you would not know the areas if you moved to a different town or city in the UK. It astonishes me that many people come over to Spain for just a week or two in order to buy property. This will probably be the second biggest investment you have, after your home in the UK. If you are moving to Spain permanently, then it will probably be (the) biggest investment you have. Take your time. Consider these issues.

THE TOURISTS

We lived in a beautiful apartment in a place called Riviera del Sol. This is next to Calahonda, between Fuengirola and Marbella. Riviera is an extremely nice place and we were delighted with the apartment we had found so we signed up for the standard eleven month rental contract. There were about thirty apartments in this relatively new complex and ours was on the second floor of three, at the end. I prefer to go for an end apartment wherever possible as there is only chance of neighbour noise coming through one side wall. This was a complex where owners either lived themselves, used the apartment for their own holiday use, or in a couple of cases were let out on long term contracts to people like ourselves who live here. We had only been in the apartment for a few weeks when one morning, around 2.00 a.m., there was a complete riot going on around the pool which was below our balcony.

What the hell! We looked out and there were five or six tourists, pissed out of their heads, diving in the pool, singing, and being sick behind the bushes – great! After a couple of nights of the same I phoned the lady who owned our apartment and told her about this problem. 'Oh yes' she said, 'the people who own number whatever decided to advertise it on the Internet for holiday lets.' Tourists came and went and within a few months other owners had decided to do the same in order to generate extra cash from their holiday investment. It was like a circus. Now I don't have anything against tourists enjoying themselves, I used to be one myself. However, when you live here the last thing you want is that lot kicking off through the night when you have to get up for work the next day. It is very common for owners to let their apartments out for holiday lets. Be aware of this whether you are looking to buy for your own use or looking to rent long term. It can make your life absolute hell, particularly during the summer months.

THE DOGS

You may think you are safe by renting or purchasing a villa whether large or small, depending on your budget. Here again, it is not something you would normally look for in the UK, but people over here who live in villas seem to have this hang up about having to own one or more large dogs. You will probably look at a villa during the day. The sun is shining; the villa has its own private garden, possibly a pool, what could be better. Complete privacy, peace and tranquility. Wrong! Visit the property again during the night. Do this for a few nights at different times. I can almost guarantee that once you get out of your car alsations, rotweillers, boxers, you name it, will explode into a thunderous roar and wake the whole bloody street up – it's true!

SPANISH OR BRITISH?

You may not have any pre conceived ideas about

whether you would prefer to live amongst Brits, Spanish or a mixture of both. It's your shout. Different complexes attract different types of people. If it is on or near a golf course, then inevitably you will be amongst fellow golfers. There are urbanizations which are a mixture of everything including Dutch, Danish, German, British, Spanish, a complete cross section. Then there are the predominantly British urbanizations which can be, if you are not careful, like living in a suburb of Manchester but with sunshine.

Personally, I would prefer the Spanish complex. The Spanish don't talk, they shout, but I can honestly say that in all the time we have lived amongst them we have experienced nothing but complete friendliness. If you are nice and polite to them, then they are nice and polite to you, it's simple. You will as often as not find that in a Spanish complex it is virtually empty for most of the year. They tend to use these homes purely as holiday homes and come down from Madrid, Cordoba, Seville, or wherever for the odd weekend or bank holiday. (Beware August). Spain just about closes during August and it seems like half the population of Spain descend on the Costa del Sol. What was an empty complex fills overnight and the month of August is a complete nightmare – it's like a Spanish Butlins. They rise in the morning and sit round the pool just like anyone else. Then around 2.00 p.m. everyone's gone, as though a bomb has dropped. They have disappeared, gone for their two to three hour Siesta, adults, kids, everyone. Then, around five or six o'clock, they reappear and stay up until two or three o'clock in the morning talking, well shouting actually. This is not done for offence; it is just the way they are. The best thing to do during August is to go on holiday yourself. Book into a hotel, buy treble glazing, rent out your apartment to a friend who doesn't know any better, but get the hell out. Then, come the first of September, peace, tranquility, back to normal for another eleven months – great!

COMMUNITY CHARGES

If you decide to rent, then as often as not the community charge is built into the rent, but this is not always the case. Ask before you commit yourself as this can make a considerable difference to your monthly outlay. If you decide to purchase a property on an urbanization then the community charge is one of the first things to enquire about. How much is it? What one off (ad hoc) costs can you be hit with (i.e. external painting of the apartment blocks), and by what rate/percentage can it increase per annum? It never ceases to amaze me the difference in community charges. You will generally find that living on a Spanish complex is considerably cheaper than living on a predominantly foreign complex in terms of the community charge. As an example, we presently have an attico (penthouse/top floor apartment), on a predominantly Spanish complex. It is overlooking the sea with beautifully tended gardens, two swimming pools and a tennis court. At the time of writing, our community charge was sixty euros per month. We know a couple who bought a brand new two bedroom apartment on a predominantly British complex of similar size but a couple of kilometers inland, fairly near a golf course. They were horrified to find, once they took the keys, that their community charge was two hundred and fifty euros per month! Too late, they had already bought it and did not ask the question first.

How do they justify that then – ask the question!

THE DAMP

The build quality in Spain is nothing like that in the UK. Double skin walls, no. To compound the problem, it is not uncommon to find that there is no damp proof course and pointing has apparently not yet been invented in Spain. If you look at new properties being built you will see holes all over the place in the brick work and no pointing at all. Once the outside walls are plastered and painted they look marvellous, but the holes are invariably still there below. Combine all these issues and you will have – damp in the winter.

Feeling the cold whilst indoors is the one thing that Brits drastically underestimate in Spain. Yes, most of the year the weather is fantastic but during the winter, when a wet cold spell arrives, you really do feel it more than you would in the UK, even though it is in reality considerably warmer. The house you left in the UK almost certainly had central heating, carpets and double glazing. It could be minus three degrees, but as soon as you walked through your front door you were warm and cosy. In Spain you will probably have no central heating, cold marble floor tiles instead of carpets, and if you do have double glazing it usually fits as well as a size ten boot on a size eight foot. Properties are primarily built to stay cool, not hot.

It is not always practical to do this, but wherever possible view properties in the winter, preferably during a rain storm or shortly afterwards. It is seriously difficult to find a Spanish property which does not suffer with damp, and often this is extreme. During the winter months many properties smell damp and have black patches all over the walls of at least one room. As such, colds and flu are just as prevalent in Spain as they are in the UK. Many people sleep in these damp conditions, breathing in the spores caused by the damp. There are not many days or weeks in the year when it does rain on the Costa, but when it rains, it rains heavily. Once the damp sets into the walls, that's it until the spring.

Many, if not most of the new properties being built at present will have reversible air conditioning. In other words they can be used to cool a property in the summer and heat it during the winter. Very few properties have central heating as we know it, and most put up with a stand alone electric or gas heater. The electric heaters are quite expensive to run so you will find that most people use what is, in effect, a gas bottle in a tin box. Most petrol stations sell these gas bottles and after a while you think nothing of it, but at first you cannot believe that you are trailing down the road with an empty gas bottle in order to change it. Personally I would rather pay the extra for electric heaters. The best we found were the plug in oil filled radiators, but make sure that you buy one with a built in thermostat which costs slightly more. You can leave these on low during the day and they will keep a room aired. You can then fire them up onto full when you get home. Hopefully this will limit the damp. It's probably me, but I don't trust the gas bottle heaters, they give off a smell and I have visions of waking up dead one morning.

There is the alternative of a (proper fire). Most Spanish properties are built with a real chimney in the lounge. Be careful! Unless you are in your sixties or seventies and remember the skills required for a real fire from your childhood, then you will probably set fire to your home as I nearly did when we lived in our rented villa. I thought – this will be great, buy some logs from the petrol station (I can have a pint while I'm in there), and a few old newspapers to get it going. We will not only be warm, but it will be quite romantic as well won't it – NO – go and buy an asbestos hat first. How many people these days know how to light a fire? I got my logs, old newspapers, a few twigs from outside and then lit the fire. 'Why is all the smoke coming back into the lounge?' Chris suggested I look up the chimney which isn't easy when six old copies of the Daily Mail are burning like an inferno. The

120

smoke alarm went off. 'Quick, er don't panic, er pull the paper and logs out of the fire, er have you got a stick or something because there is no way I am putting my hand in there.' As I am shouting all this, I am jogging around the lounge like a mad dog in all directions but not actually going anywhere. 'Quick, whack that bastard smoke alarm 'cos it's doing my head in.' 'I would but I can't see it, in fact I can't see you either,' Chris said. This was getting serious so I legged it into the kitchen, picked up a pan, filled it with water, and then chucked it into the fire. Back to the kitchen for a refill and by this time the room was seriously full of smoke, it was a war zone, more water. We opened all the doors and windows which, from outside, must have looked as though we were electing a new Pope. 'What have we done'? We just sat outside with blackened faces and let the smoke clear. When we went back inside an hour or so later we could have cried. Apparently I had missed with one of the pans full of water and thrown it all over our video recorder. The new beige rug which Chris had recently purchased looked as if it had done a tour of the local sewerage works – twice. I was ashamed, as I had been in the Boy Scouts you know.

It's like camping, it's archaic, it's backward – but it's often as good as it gets – damp!

THE COMMUNITY UNDERGROUND CAR PARK

If you buy or rent a villa or townhouse in Spain, you are likely to get a private individual garage for your vehicle.

Many houses are built in such a way that these private garages are beneath the property and in many cases they are huge, like an aircraft hanger. People will often take advantage of this extra space and create an extra room for the children, a bar, pool room or whatever. If, on the other hand, you buy or rent an apartment then you will either get road parking or your own numbered bay within the community underground car park. Usually these will be secure from outsiders with electric gates protecting the area.

Beware – many vendettas in Spain are carried out in the community underground car park.

It could have started with noise from a stereo, slamming doors during the night, stiletto heels from the apartment above, scraping furniture on the floor, a barking dog, anything. If you speak to any Brit who has lived in Spain for a number of years, you will struggle to find one who has not either had their own vehicle damaged, or know someone who has, within the community underground car park. The favorite is sticking a knife through one or all of your tyres. This happened to my Harley Davidson, and I still don't know to this day why or by whom. A friend of Chris's son bought a gleaming bright red 3 Series BMW which understandably he was chuffed to bits with. Only two days later, he went down to the community underground car park and someone had poured a full can of paint stripper all over the bonnet. These places are usually secure from outsiders, but they are not secure from other people who live or stay on the complex. As with virtually anywhere else, there are some very nasty people down here.

THE COMMUNITY UNDERGROUND CAR PARK (GARAGE DOOR)

This is definitely something to consider. As previously mentioned, most apartment complexes have the community underground car park. Some have one single large garage door for both entry and exit. Many have two doors, one for entry and the other for exit. These are usually huge electronic doors which are opened with a 'zapper.' Beware of the apartment directly over the top of these entry and exit doors. You will be asleep and throughout the night these bloody great things are banging open and closed making it virtually impossible to get a decent night's sleep. Avoid these apartments like the plague.

BEWARE THE (FINDERS FEE)

If you are looking to rent an apartment or villa long term (eleven month contract); you will be lucky to get away without paying a finders fee. Most property owners who are looking to rent their apartment or villa will use a letting agent. You will see a property advertised with a stated rent, contact the agent enquiring about the property, and they will then show you it. If you decide to take the property you will inevitably be asked to pay up front—

1 months deposit (at least), sometimes two.

1 months rent in advance

+ 1 months rent as a 'finders fee'

The finders fee is also sometimes called a management fee and is payable only once on each let. That is at the outset prior to moving in. Do not fall for the same assumption that I did. We rented a villa on the road up to Mijas village and were there for nearly two years. At the end of the first eleven month contract, we spoke to the agent and informed him that we would like to stay for a further eleven month contract. 'Fine,' said the agent. 'I will draw up another contract for signature.' Stupidly, very stupidly, I said, so that will be the first months rent up front again, plus the management fee? 'Yes, that's right,' said the agent. We paid the money and spent another happy eleven months in our villa before moving on. Strange as it may sound, it was another six or nine months before I found out that I shouldn't have paid the management fee again. It was my own stupid fault as it was me who put the words into his mouth, and of course he agreed. One thousand four hundred euros. 'Thank you very much – Mr. Stupid!'

As often as not when you decide to leave the property you have rented, you will not get the deposit back. They will make any excuse up you care to name such as, 'that paint wasn't scratched,' or 'that tile there wasn't cracked when you moved in,' anything. You would do well to assume that you will lose the deposit and write it off over the eleven months of your contract. If you do get it back, as you have been lucky enough to drop on an (honorable) agent, then look upon that as a bonus.

WHO PAYS FOR REPAIRS—YOU DO!

If you rent a property and something breaks, then more often than not, it is YOU and not the owner who is expected to pay for it repairing. In the UK things are generally the other way around. For instance, if the water heater packs in and you phone your agent in order to inform him of the fact, the reply you get will usually be—'then fix it!' It may be that the washing machine has broken down, 'then fix it.' It's a shock. You don't expect that, you assume that the owner will sort it out. He doesn't! 'My brother is a heating engineer,' or 'I can get someone out quickly,' says the agent. Read into that what you will. A slice on top for the agent again eh!'

THE 'SNAGGING' LIST

When you buy a brand new property and you finally get the key, which is normally considerably later than agreed, you are asked to spend a little time there and have a good look around. Try the appliances, check the fit of the doors, make sure the loo's flush, and generally check that everything is to your satisfaction. Take this to the extreme! Rev everything up to breaking point, turn it off, and then rev it up again. Make absolutely sure that everything is in full working order because if you don't, then trying to get things fixed afterwards is more or less a none starter. You will be very fortunate if you do not find something which requires attention. Once you find faults and generate your (snagging list), how do you get the jobs done. You will probably be in the UK. Many developers will not hold your keys once they have been handed over to you. They do not want to take responsibility if someone goes in there. So how do the workmen get in? These outstanding jobs can take months to sort out and I have known people who have been literally tearing their hair out not knowing where to turn next. They are so frustrated that they sell the bloody thing before they have had one holiday in it.

This is not the UK, and in most Spanish businesses, customer service has not yet been invented. I am not trying to say that this is the norm, but I highlight below the experience of a friend of mine. It may not be the norm, but it is certainly not unusual.

The couple in question live in the UK and are keen golfers. They bought a brand new two bedroom, two bathroom apartment near the Torrequebrada golf course. They got so frustrated being in the UK and not being able to get any sense or action from the developer that they asked for our help. We agreed to hold a key for them and try to get the outstanding jobs done at this end. Letting in the workmen, if and when they arrived, and being present whilst work was being carried out. They had bought the property as many people do (off plan), and it was due to be completed during March 2004. They actually got their keys at the end of October. They then visited the apartment in order to compile the snagging list mid November. A whole new nightmare began. Chris and I were constantly making telephone calls to the developer as were the owners from the UK. After a while these people decided they were not making any progress whatsoever with the developers, so they then went to the real estate company whom they had purchased through. In order to highlight this couple's plight, I duplicate below, word for word apart from names, which I have changed, an e-mail they sent to a senior manager at the real estate company in question –

Attention of Jose Garcia – Sales Manager Snag Estates

I find myself in this situation out of desperation and have written this E mail due to the fact that as we English say I am running around in circles getting nowhere.

This is no reflection on your company or your representative Mike Hammond from whom we purchased the property who is a credit to Snag Estates.

LET'S BEGIN

June 2002 – Arrived in Spain viewed various show houses with Mike decided to purchase off plan property in Torrequebrada

Paid deposit, property due for completion March 2004 everything ok so far.

Visited property through various stages and was

told property would be completed late March 2004. Completion was put back to June 2004 so I booked holiday for August assuming this would give sufficient time over June completion date.

My brother and family also booked for August i.e. paid for flights. Both holidays were ruined and we had to find alternative accommodation at the last minute, at our expense due to the fact that the property was again delayed. We were told completion would be 23rd September.

October 8th – 15th. Had holiday booked with friends, again had to book alternative accommodation at last minute due to property still not being completed.

October 18th – 25th. Wife and friends had to find alternative accommodation at last minute due to property still not being completed.

October 26th. At last collected keys 7 months late but suppose it is Spain.

November 18th – My wife and 3 friends visited apartment to compile a snagging list which had to be given to the developers before 24th Nov. The list was compiled and presented to Maria in the office on Sat. 19th November 2004.

December 11th – 12th – Visited for weekend – nothing had been done, all faults still outstanding, stayed in apartment with no electricity as we had been told this would be connected or we would be supplied with builders electric as a temporary measure but we had neither and as it was a weekend, nothing could be done.

December 26th – 1st January – Visited for 1 week with friends, electric had been connected but nothing on the snagging list had been done. Our friends in Spain were in constant contact with the developers but were getting no help or response from them and in fact they were telling them lies about when and what was to be done.

28th January – 30th January – Visited for weekend, again nothing has been done from the snagging list and we have had to add two other items to the list since it was first presented. At each visit we go to the office and request that our repairs are carried out. We are starting to lose patience.

12th February – Spoke to Mike to ask if he can help by putting some pressure on, he receives no assurances when work will be completed, says speak to you Monday.

Please note Mike only became involved last couple of weeks due to desperation and has been nothing but efficient and helpful as possible but we are still getting nowhere.

Throughout this total nightmare I have been continually lied to by Anton and Maria at the Torrequebrada offices, financially incurred extra flights and accommodation, sat in the apartment with no electricity, slept in beds fully clothed due to heating not working in bedrooms, shutters that do not work. Myself and Mike have spoken to the Lawyer who told us if work is not completed in ten days we have the right to have the work finished and recharge the developers. This date has now passed and Lawyer is not returning E mails or phone calls from my friends in Spain.

I think I have been very patient uptill now and will be returning to Spain on the 24th February with important clients of mine and I am asking you as my agent to intervene and endeavour to have these problems rectified at no cost to myself.

I have recommended your company to one of my colleagues who did purchase a resale from yourselves. I respectfully request help in this matter with your Aftersales Department.

The snagging list is as follows :-

1. The hot water boiler leaks and according to their engineer requires a complete replacement. Water has to be switched off when not in use as leak is so bad.
2. The microwave oven does not work, there appears to be no power going to it.
3. The 'hot' aircon works in the lounge but does not blow through to the bedrooms.
4. The patio window shutter in the second bedroom is wired the wrong way round i.e. when you press shutter up button it goes down and viceversa.
5. The main patio window shutter in the lounge does not work at all and it is permanently in the down position, as such there is no natural light in the lounge area and you cannot access the patio only through the bedroom.

I await your prompt response.

Well that did it. Someone at a very high level within the real estate company obviously spoke to a director at the developers. I received a call only a few days later, asking if I could be at the apartment the following afternoon in order for someone to view the problems and rectify them. Great, things are going to get fixed. Wrong! As agreed, I arrived the following afternoon and our contact at the developers, Maria, turned up with these two guys wearing black designer suits, shiny shoes, and sunglasses. I thought they were The Blues Brothers. Maria explained that these two guys were actually directors of the development company and wanted to view what all the fuss was about. I said; hang on a minute Maria, you mean these guys are only looking. The jobs are not actually going to be done today. 'Well possibly, if they can fix anything themselves they will do.' Yeah right, in Armani suits and sunglasses, I don't think so! The next thing I know, these guys are standing on dining room chairs. One was poking around with the air vents for the aircon, and the other one was trying to prise the microwave out of its housing using a pen. 'Have you got a screwdriver they can borrow?' Well, yes, I suppose I will have one in the tool kit for my car. I lent them a VW screwdriver. They forced the aircon vent in each bedroom off the ceiling. Apparently there is a fin inside which was in the wrong position, not allowing air into these rooms. Fine, one job done. With regard to the other problems, they agreed that these actually were problems. Suited and booted they then left. I had another word with Maria who told me that they would now have to pay someone to come and rectify the faults at a later date. A new boiler was required, but it would be virtually impossible to get the company who installed them to return. They would take one out of another apartment which had not yet been sold. Presumably at some point down the line, the poor sods who eventually bought this other apartment would then go through the same procedure, chasing a new boiler. The developers would get their own technician to view the electric shutter and look at the microwave also. Sure enough, after making a number of calls to their office, they asked me to be there again one afternoon. I arrived and waited for their (technician). He arrived with another member of the sales staff with whom I had spoken on the phone. We will call this other sales person Marco. The technician looked at the microwave and confirmed that there was no electricity going into it but this was not something he could do himself. He then dismantled the electric window shutter in the lounge with a large pen knife and showed me the badly bent girder around which the shutter winds. They described it as a girder because it was load bearing, but the bloody thing was only made out of aluminium. It didn't look as if it would take the weight of a dead dog. 'That requires a new one and it will have to be ordered from the manufacturer,' he said. The other shutter in the bedroom was a two minute job changing the wires round in the switch. Not a terrific amount of progress there then.

Marco told me that Spain is completely different to the UK as most jobs during a build are sub contracted. Once jobs are complete, the sub contractors disappear and it is virtually impossible to get them back to rectify problems. I said, why don't you hold monies back then as security for them repairing faults. 'Oh we do – five per cent. But all they do then is build the five per cent into their price at the outset and then walk away. They are not interested.' But surely that gives them a bad reputation and they don't get any more work from you? 'No, they all do it, so they are all as bad as each other.' – Eh! But this is disgraceful, what about customer service, after sales, it doesn't exist. 'I know' he said, 'it's terrible isn't it.' Wrong answer pal, I must calm down now as I am about to smack him. It isn't even my apartment! I told Marco that in the UK this just would not happen, and that a company operating like this would quickly go out of business. 'Yes' he says, 'but this is Spain and it's not like that, things take much longer.'

Oh that's alright then!

After more telephone calls and two more visits, the jobs were all done. If my friend had tried to do this alone from the UK, he would not have stood a chance. Beware of these issues, think it through, and take your time. If you are to invest your hard earned money into brand new Spanish property, it is vital that you get it right first time.

I have known people who have spent not hundreds, but thousands of pounds on flights over here in order to try and get things done face to face. The telephone is a fob off accessory. Even when they do come over, invariably the work man doesn't turn up or a new part is required from the manufacturer. The game starts again. If the problems are serious enough for you to be unable to stay in your own apartment, you then have the extra cost of accommodation. It's expensive, it's frustrating. In extreme cases people wish they had never set eyes on their bloody apartment. What started off as a dream is now a complete liability. 'It's more bother than it's worth, it's a pain in the arse.' GET RID!

CYNICAL PROPERTY DEVELOPERS AND BUILDERS

When purchasing property over here, there are two popular sayings –

1) If there is any spare land around it, then you can almost guarantee that it will be built on. In other words, if you have a view now, then the chances are that you will not have a view shortly.

2) If you cannot touch it and see it, then don't buy it.

A very good friend of ours bought a brand new town house in Los Pacos which is just on the outskirts of Fuengirola. He bought the end one of six. It has four bedrooms, an enormous underground garage and a shared pool. The house was in an elevated position on a hillside and the view from his front terrace was magnificent. The sea was about a mile away and you could see Fuengirola promenade, boats the lot. He was quite rightly very proud of his new house, particularly the views. On an evening he would sit on the terrace with a glass of wine or a beer and look at Fuengirola from a distance, all lit up, beautiful. Once all the houses in the row were finished and sold, the same builder he had bought from moved equipment onto the land right in front of his terrace. They dug foundations out, and walls began to grow. 'That wasn't on the plans when I looked at them.' After not too long, a wall was completely blocking out his view. It quickly became evident that they were building another row of town houses directly in front of his, at right angles to it. In other words his terrace and lounge now look onto the gable end of another house. That is quite literally what he can see now. It's not right. They wouldn't get away with it in the UK, but this is not the UK!

There is an area between Fuengirola and La Cala where a particular Spanish family own seven small houses all in a row, side by side. These are in fact small bungalows and are predominantly occupied by family members. There is the mother, son number one and family, son number two and family, daughter and family etc. etc. A couple of these bungalows are rented out on long term contracts. There was an area of elevated spare land behind these houses which they also owned. The family sold this spare land to a developer for the construction of a number of very large, very expensive semi detached villas. Prior to the land sale, the family secured planning permission to put another floor on some or all of the original bungalows. They then did nothing. The developer moved in, proceeded to build the new properties and they were all sold very quickly off plan. They are very nice. The people who bought these new houses did not have a clue that the bungalows directly in front of them had permission to build another floor on top. As I write this book the houses are almost ready for occupation and no move has yet been made to put another floor on any of the existing bungalows. They will wait until all the monies have been paid and the new purchasers have moved in. Then – bingo – bang – work will commence, in effect blocking a good part of the view directly in front of their new houses. There is absolutely nothing these people will be able to do about it as planning permission was already in place prior to the construction of their property.

It is cynical, it is nasty, and it is premeditated. Unfortunately it is not unusual and the developers don't give a damn.

Golf properties sell for a premium for obvious reasons. Next to the golf course, sometimes looking over one of the greens. Now that's got snob value hasn't it. You buy a villa or apartment and pay a large premium for what they call (front line). In other words, uninterrupted views over the golf course. Normally on the original plans, front line properties are shown and built quite a distance from the course itself, 'you don't want a golf ball through your front window do you' – of course not. Once the front line properties are built and sold, you will often see another row of properties going up in front of the front line. The front line has suddenly become the second line. Sometimes this will happen again. Your premium front line property is now three lines back with a beautiful view of the back of other houses or apartments. Now that really is a dirty trick, but believe me it happens. Watch this space. At some point a developer will probably build over the whole bloody golf course once all the properties have been sold!

We were developer victims, indirectly. Chris and I became involved in a Spanish bad dream when we bought our apartment. It is so easily done. You don't see it coming because you don't know what you are looking for. They say in the UK that moving or purchasing a house is second only to divorce in terms of stress and pressure. I would suggest that moving or purchasing a property in Spain can be way beyond any divorce pressure you care to name. We first looked at our apartment in June 2004. It is a two bedroom, two bathroom, penthouse/attico (they are posh names for a top floor flat)! It has a frontal sea view which is in your face when you open the curtains in the morning. From the balcony, there is a spiral staircase going up to the roof garden which is the full area of the apartment. The views are stunning. At one side of the apartment is fresh air and at the other side is the stair well so there is no chance of neighbour TV or hi-fi noise as nobody is joined on. That is difficult to find, very difficult indeed. We immediately fell in love with it, and as we had spent three years looking, we were convinced that this was definitely the one for us. We had heard that these Spanish people were selling through a friend of ours, but there was no 'for sale' sign in evidence. When we spoke to them they explained that they were having a house built and that it would not be complete until December. They were not actually looking to sell just yet. As we really wanted this property we agreed to talk again during September. Sure enough, when September arrived we went to see them again and had another look around just to make sure. Yes, we wanted it. The jousting began over price but there was no way these people would budge an inch. They wouldn't drop it one euro and as we didn't want them to put it on the market, we agreed to pay the full asking price. It hurt but we had spent three years looking, albeit casually, at every kind of property you can imagine. This one had everything we wanted and more. The house these people were having built was behind schedule (what a shock), and rather than a December completion, they were now looking at January or February at the very latest – honest! They wanted to leave the completion date open, but knowing Spanish builders as we did, there was no way that we were going to agree to that. We weren't happy about it, but reluctantly agreed to have the completion on the 31st March. This gave them a month buffer over and above the end of February very very very latest – honest, completion date given by the builders. We met at our Gestoria's office, signed the contract and handed over the standard

10% deposit. We began looking at new furniture, patio furniture, light fittings, and all the other things people look at whilst waiting to move house. Meanwhile the end of March loomed. Around mid February, the guy we were buying our apartment from contacted us and asked for a meeting. We turned up at a café he had suggested and initially he just danced around the subject we knew he was going to raise. It had to come and it did, 'our house is still behind schedule and we would like to change the contract again. We want to move the completion date back seven, eight, or possibly nine weeks.' What, is he taking the piss or is it April fools day! No, he was deadly serious. Chris and I looked at each other – no, no, no, no. He insisted that we had a meeting at the office of our Gestoria very quickly. We agreed as this had to be sorted. A couple of nights later there we were, and our Gestoria was great. The guy we were buying from and his wife got so excited we couldn't believe it. I could only follow some of the conversation because once the Spanish (go on one), they speak so quickly that it is impossible to detect the breaks between words. Chris and I just sighed and looked out of the window, totally disinterested. Eventually our Gestoria spoke. 'These people are refusing to leave at the end of March as stated in the contract signed by both parties. They insist on an extension of up to three months. I have told them that if they will not move on this, and if you do not agree, then they are in breach of the contract therefore owing to you DOUBLE the deposit you paid them. In Spain if a seller takes a deposit from a purchaser and then breaks his or her contract, then they have to pay the purchaser double the deposit amount. These people called the bluff. They wouldn't move on anything so we danced around again, trying to find a compromise. There were all kinds of things to consider, not least the fact that we had already given a months notice on our rented apartment. There was also the mortgage, how long would the bank hold it for? We agreed to meet again the following evening after we had discussed it further together and our Gestoria had spoken to the bank regarding our mortgage. The following evening, off they go again, shouting, waving their arms around, and banging papers on the desk. Chris and I just crossed our legs, folded our arms, and looked out of the window; just let them get on with it. If this had taken place in the UK you can imagine one of the blokes just standing up and slotting the other one, job done! Our Gestoria spoke again, 'the best compromise I can agree upon is for the completion contract to be changed to the end of May, two months. These people will not get any more money until that point. Then, the keys MUST be handed over as the mortgage will have gone through and the property will be owned by you.' It was not what Chris and I were looking for but we really wanted this apartment and were not prepared to lose it for the sake of two months. Okay, we could dig our heels in and they would have to pay us back double our deposit but in the scheme of things this wasn't a fortune. Oh bollocks, we will wait! That means from the first time we viewed this place to moving in will have been eleven months. Sometimes you have to take a deep breath and back off. Being stubborn can make you feel better initially, but cost you in the long run.

All because the Developer was late, very late——————again!

BE CAREFUL!

Buying a property over here often involves (black money) as it does when buying a business, but for different reasons. If you find a property you wish to purchase for (say) 300,000 euros, it will possibly go through as a sale for (say) 220,000 euros for tax reasons. The transaction will go through at 220,000 and you will then get the old briefcase out again. You will fill it with 80,000 euros in cash, put a baseball bat down your trouser leg just in case, and then give it to the seller (the money that is). Don't worry, because if and when you come to sell the property, you may do exactly the same.

THE PROPERTY MANAGERS

The majority of British owned properties on the Costa del Sol are unoccupied for most of the year. Some owners rent out their properties on long term (11 month) contracts to people who live here. Others rent theirs out on the Internet, through agents, in the newspaper, or whatever, as holiday lets. Most owners use the property for their own holiday use with occasional family and close friends. Many of these people have a (property manager). There are lots and lots of property management companies and there are some excellent ones. There are also some really bad ones with unscrupulous people playing tricks you would find difficult to believe. Many of the large real estate companies offer property management facilities. There are also hundreds of small private property managers who invariably start off with a couple of properties and then grow it into a decent size business. Property managers are there to look after your investment whilst you are in the UK. They will visit the property in order to make sure everything is in order, they will clean it prior to visitors arriving, clean it after visitors have left, sometimes offer to provide pre visit shopping, and be there in case someone locks themselves out or breaks something. If you use the right people then property managers are a great asset and you can hopefully feel comfortable that your investment is safe in your absence. It is imperative that if someone holds a key to your property that you can trust them 100%. That it not easy!

First of all we will take the large real estate companies.

Let's just say that you bought your property through (James) at one of the major real estate companies on the coast. You have been delighted with the service you received from James. When he offers you their property management service the trust factor is already there. You go with them – why not? The problem is that it will not be James personally who visits and cleans your apartment. It will be someone, probably a sub contracted cleaner, who actually does the work. That's a key in another set of hands. For all you know, and it happens, this cleaning person is letting his or her relatives or friends stay in your property when it's empty. You wouldn't know would you – how could you?

Then there are the small independent property management companies. If you go with one of these, they will have to hold a key. As in the UK, you can go into one of many shops and get a key cut in minutes. You would be absolutely horrified if you knew how many apartments, town houses, and villas are lived in at some point without the owner in the UK having a clue. What's going on? You don't know – you are in the UK. People with access to property keys sometimes let their friends, parents, children or whatever, stay in YOUR apartment, free of charge. Sometimes they will actually charge for the privilege and make good money out of YOUR investment.

We knew an Irish lady who had an apartment in Calahonda. She had used a local property management company and to the best of her knowledge, everything was going fine. During one of her many visits to the apartment she happened to mention to her property managers that her apartment insurance was due for payment. She would have to renew it while she was over. 'Oh, don't you bother with that. Leave the money with us and we will sort it out for you as we get much better rates. All part of the service.'

A few weeks passed when she received a call in Ireland from one of her neighbours in Calahonda. They informed her that the people in the apartment above hers had left a bath running and completely flooded her premises. This lady jumped on a plane and was horrified to see the mess when she arrived, lounge suite, beds, the lot – ruined! She then proceeded to the property managers and explained the mess that they were not even aware of. Obviously they had not been anywhere near her apartment for some time which is what they were being paid for. 'Well at least I'm insured.' 'Er – well no actually, we never paid the premium.'

These are the kind of people that some owners are dealing with.

It is always a good idea to make friends with people in neighbouring properties. This is sometimes not easy as you may only be staying in your property two, three of maybe four times a year. The more people you get talking to the better. You need not be best friends with them, but at least if you have had a conversation or two with them they will keep an eye on your property whilst they are there and you are not. It works both ways. Make the suggestion to them that you reciprocate the arrangement. Even suggest that they put a short note under your door whilst you are away, informing you of any visitors. Swap telephone numbers. It is in everyone's interest at the end of the day and if you can help each other to avoid the unpaying guest, so much the better. This is not being a nosey neighbour; it's just common sense, and well worth doing. Always go with a recommendation from a fellow owner who has had consistently good service, for a reasonable amount of time, from a property manager. If you have any doubt whatsoever that a key may be in the hands of someone else, then change the lock immediately. It is not expensive, and the small investment could save you a fortune.

THE CLEAR OUT

The worse case scenario of your key being in the wrong hands is (the clear out). The clear out is certainly not a common occurrence, but it does happen. Your key is lent to someone, possibly a sub contract cleaner or a work man. This person nips down to the local hardware shop or shopping complex and gets a key cut. A few days later, or possibly a few weeks later, that person pulls up with a van and clears the property out, furniture, TV, DVD, the lot. The first you are likely to know about this is when you next visit. What are you going to sort out in a week or two. Not a lot, some holiday eh!

HOW UNLUCKY CAN YOU GET

You can take all the precautions available to you and still be the victim of plain bad luck. Two people we knew bought a first floor apartment in the Dona Sofia complex at the west side of Fuengirola. They purchased this property and then returned to the UK with a view to moving over here permanently at some point in the fairly near future. Literally three weeks after returning to the UK, this guy was having a haircut in his local barbers shop when over the radio came the news that 'a bomb had gone off in Fuengirola.' He turned to the barber and said, 'ha ha, knowing my bloody luck that bomb will have gone off right outside my new apartment.' The next morning he bought a newspaper and there it was. 'Oh bollocks!' A frontal view of his pride and joy apartment with the shit blown out of it. The bomb had gone off outside the Las Piramides Hotel which just happened to be straight opposite his new apartment. He was insured, but it took him forever to get the money out of the insurance company and rectify the scene from Beirut. A bomb had totaled his new apartment. If he had walked into a bookies office the day before, what odds could he have got against that happening?

Bad luck, plain and simple, you can't allow for it!

SPANISH PROPERTY – BE CAREFUL!

CHAPTER SIX

Get a (proper job) on the Costa del Sol

You will struggle.

People moving to Spain who are without the financial resources to buy a business of their own, present themselves with the task of finding a job. Finding a job is not too difficult, but finding a (proper) job is very difficult indeed.

Wages over here are nowhere near what they are in the UK. For instance, if you can get a job in a bar or restaurant you will be looking at being paid around 5 euros per hour. Depending on the exchange rate, but working on 1.40 to the pound, that is £3.57 per hour. You wouldn't get out of bed for that in the UK. I have known people who have taken bar jobs out of desperation at 3.00 euros per hour which is £2.14. Can you live on that, I doubt it. Not even out here. If you do secure a job, it is very difficult to find an employer who is willing to put you on a proper employment contract. There is the cost to an employer of National Insurance which comes with a contract and small businesses are rarely prepared to pay this. Then there is the cost of holiday pay and sick pay. Employees also have far more employment rights in Spain so it is very difficult and expensive to (get rid) of someone, particularly if they are on a full time contract.

As the Costa del Sol is geared to tourism and property development, then by definition many of the jobs which are on offer are within these sectors. In the UK, if you pick up a local newspaper and look at the situations vacant section there will probably be a massive diversification of jobs such as secretaries, motor mechanics, local government officers, printers, electricians, plumbers, you name it. If you look at one of the local Costa del Sol English language newspapers however, you will see a different story completely. Most advertised positions are for tele sales staff (commission based), real estate sales staff (commission based), timeshare sales (commission based), bar work (around 5 euros per hour) – that's it! The commission based jobs are jam tomorrow jobs. How can you budget your living costs if you haven't got a clue how much you will earn, if anything. In some cases people take these jobs, do a few deals, but then find that their commission is not forthcoming. 'Goodbye, get out.' 'But

I thought I was doing okay. I have spent a month working for you and I have done three deals. You have not paid me my commission.' 'That's right, what are you going to do about it. You are not officially employed here, goodbye.' It happens!

If you were lucky enough to secure a position with a reputable company who said they were prepared to put you on a contract, the chances of you seeing six months employment are remote. Many companies will take on staff (say a receptionist or secretary), and tell the person that they are on a trial but that there will be an official contract available if both parties are happy with each other. This trial period will move on and on but hardly ever beyond six month. Bang bang–your dead–some half brain excuse and you are down the road ready for the next person. No contract, no rights.

Chris's daughter, Justine, suffered endless times with the (five monther). She liked the jobs and as far as she was aware they liked her, but no way were they going to tie themselves into a full time contract–goodbye!

NO WORK, NO MONEY!

Spain is not the UK. If you move over here and do not work, then you can sleep in the street or on the beach. There is no going down to the dole office and picking up a GIRO, forget it. That's fine, most people have no problem with that whatsoever.

It is not easy. If you come here to retire then you would

struggle to find a better life. If you come here to open a business and make a success of it, then the same applies. However, if you come here to open a business and fail or you just arrive hoping to find a (proper job), then you will inevitably be very disappointed indeed and struggle badly. If you want to even get close to securing a proper job in southern Spain within an office environment, then fluent Spanish is a must. Not just verbal. You will have to be able to read, write and type in Spanish. If you have that ability then you have a chance.

It is not easy to come down here and earn a decent living, not easy at all. Understand that before you make the move!

CHAPTER SEVEN

Southern Spain is a great place to live but Christ, it can be annoying!

They say down here that you should never try to achieve more than one thing per day. I laughed at this when we first arrived but believe me, it is true. Going back to the old (customer service) thing, us Brits are used to going into somewhere, being served, get out as quickly as possible and then on to the next task. Life is fast, if you want it, do it, what's next? In Spain life is not like that. Progress has been, and still is being made, but there is a massive mountain to climb in certain areas of business. The culture over here is different, what's the rush, orderly queue – what's one of those?

THE BANKS

The greatest frustration for Brits living in Spain are the Banks. Banks are a massive topic of conversation and they are the institutions that people love to hate. Not that they bombard you with junk mail or that they are constantly trying to lend you money, but most transactions are carried out by a personal visit to the bank. This is very much a cash society and as such, a visit to the bank is totally necessary for many things.

Now don't get me wrong, most of the bank staff are lovely people, it's just that they have got their priorities completely wrong. There is a definite batting order with bank staff which is apparent as soon as you walk into many bank branches. There may be two or three cashier desks but invariably there will only be one which is occupied by a junior member of staff. The queue (of sorts) will be twenty deep reaching the outside door and behind the single cashier could be six or seven suited staff trying to look important, laughing, joking, drinking coffee, and not one of them will even think of occupying a vacant cashiers desk. You get the impression that this would be beneath them. The time it takes each person at the cash desk is also much longer than you would experience in the UK because many people are depositing multiple bills in cash or putting cash from their business into the bank. It seems to take forever.

One small branch of a particular bank I needed to visit every month had this old guy on the cash desk who we called (fish face). He was the most miserable bastard you could ever imagine meeting. He was slow, ignorant and his keyboard skills none existent as he seemed to input everything about five times before he got it right. On top of that, if there was anyone in that he knew then he would spend ten minutes talking to them, but if he didn't know you, then he was just plain old fish face. One day I made my monthly visit and there, behind the cash desk, was the guy who I had previously assumed to be the manager as he was never doing anything. Fish face must be on holiday or ill (nothing trivial I hope). This manager guy was brilliant. There were four people in front of me and he dispensed with the lot of us in a few minutes. If he was the manager, then he must have known just how crap this fish face guy was so why keep him—sack him, trash him, throw him into the sea, he's a liability.

If you meet up with friends in town and you tell them that you are going to the bank, I can guarantee that they will fall about laughing. That's just the way it is, and if someone opened a proper bank in Spain they would clean up.

We had an account with one particular bank and on a visit to the dreaded cash desk I was informed that they now had Internet banking and would I like to discuss it with one of the behind the desk people? Wow—space age—just what I have been waiting for—about time. Yes, of course I would. I was shown to this very nice gentleman's desk who explained this (new) technology of which he was very proud. I received a series of codes and a quick demo' on his screen which made me feel that I could now probably cut down on my branch visits. A couple of days later I went into their Internet banking and viewed our account with no problems whatsoever. As it happened, shortly afterwards, I wanted to set up a standing order so I was delighted that I wouldn't have to queue at the branch in order to do so. Having played around with the system for a while I thought, that's all I can do, look at my account. I am no genius on a computer but I am no slouch either. Try as I may, I could not do anything other than view our account status. I telephoned the bank and spoke to a lady about how I could use their Internet banking for transactions etc. 'Oh no, I am afraid you cannot do that. All you can do at present is view your own account status.' Oh well that's really useful – thanks a bunch – its archaic!

Banks also charge high fees in Spain. Every time you receive a statement there are charges for this, charges for that, and some banks actually charge you for putting money in – what's all that about? We found the best way was to keep our money in a UK account and just transfer it over as and when required. The more we could achieve over the telephone and Internet the better.

THE SIESTA

Opening hours in Spanish businesses can be confusing. The (Siesta) is part of Spanish life and many shops and businesses still close for two or three hours during the afternoon. Inevitably if something goes wrong, you require quick help, or you run out of something and need replacements immediately, it is Siesta time. You can bank on it 'if you have time.' It is 2.30 p.m. and you need to speak to someone regarding business or money. You have no chance, no chance at all. You might be lucky and catch them at 4 o'clock, but it is more likely to be 5 o'clock. In years gone by you can understand working people wanting to get out of the summer heat for a couple of hours sleep and then re-emerging at 5 o'clock to work in a more tolerable temperature. At present most offices, shops and businesses have air conditioning anyway, and many people commute considerable distances to work. Siesta is tradition; it is the Spanish way of life. We live in their country and respect that, but I just cannot get my head round say a shop assistant, finishing at 2 o'clock every afternoon, getting into his or her car, driving home, getting into bed for a sleep and then getting back to work for 5 o'clock. How much sleep would they get anyway – what's the point?

RAIN STOPS PLAY – I MEAN WORK!

One element which grinds the wheels of industry to a halt is the rain. If it rains, you try and get someone to fix something – forget it.

We once had a problem with the hot water in a villa we rented. It was during a particularly wet spell in the winter and we spoke to the agent who promised to get a guy out to fix it. This particular agent used the same Spanish guy for just about any job requiring attention in any of his properties. No hot water during a cold spell is not pleasant and having waited in all the following day the guy never arrived – what a shock! This went on for four days during which time we were boiling kettles, pans and anything else we could lay our hands on. When he did eventually arrive I asked where the hell he had been as we had been boiling water just to have a wash. 'Oh it's been raining so I couldn't work' – Eh!

Roads turn into rivers and rivers turn into waterfalls, everything stops! Storm drains, what are those?

THE RECEIPT GAME

An example of the silly things you can fall for is the (lack of receipt) game which is a favourite played by many Spaniards. I fell for this one but got away with it thankfully.

When we first opened our business we were introduced by the previous owners to an English guy who was an insurance broker. They had got their business insurance through him and he was recommended. This guy gave us a price and as one does, we obtained two or three alternative quotations from insurance companies we had seen advertised in the local press. His price was there or thereabouts so we went with him and arranged to meet him at the offices of a fairly large insurance company in Fuengirola in order to fill out the necessary forms. This we did, paid the cash, and walked out with a certificate. Not uncommon for over here but this insurance broker disappeared and so when the insurance was due again the following year, I telephoned the insurance company in order to secure a price for the renewal. Fortunately there was a Scandinavian woman working in the office who spoke English so she gave me the details of the premium and we agreed that I would call in later that week. When I got to the office I searched out the Scandinavian lady and she told me to go to the Spanish guy sat opposite her, give my name and he would sort me out – fine. I gave my name, he found the insurance certificate, I handed over the money and away I go. A few days later I received a phone call from the same insurance company asking me when I was going to pay the premium. Pardon, I have paid the premium, I paid it when I collected the certificate. They were absolutely adamant that 'according to their records' the premium had not been paid. That evening I went round to the offices again and spoke to the guy who I took to be in charge and he spoke a little English. 'No sir, the premium has not been paid. Do you have a receipt'? Hang on a minute; I have the insurance certificate, its here, look. How come I have got this if I haven't paid the premium, you wouldn't have given me this without having first received the money. 'No sorry, we issue renewal certificates automatically, sometimes through the post and if the premium is not paid shortly afterwards then we assume the customer does not require renewal and cancel the policy.' But you must reconcile monies at the end of each day, surely your takings must have been up that day, you must keep records. He shrugged his shoulders – couldn't give a toss. You bastards – I've been striped! I go over to the guy who I gave the cash to and he just shook his head and waved me away. That was it, I'd lost it, I hate being robbed. We were talking about a few hundred euros here, not the price of a pint. I marched over to the Scandi' lady and was shouting by now – I'd gone into full John Cleese mode – it was only a few days ago, you must remember, I came in to pay a premium and you asked me to go and see that guy there, yes him, the one who is keeping his head down. 'Yes I do remember you and yes, I did see you pay him' – thank Christ for that! The lady spoke to the manager in Spanish and his expression suddenly changed from calm to very annoyed. He went over to the cash guy and gave him a right ear bashing then turned to me and said in broken English, 'sorry there has been a mistake, all is okay and we hope to see you again next year.' **Fat f-----g chance of that!** That 'Pedro the Bandit' cash guy had trousered my money and how many other times had he done it. Whatever you buy or pay for, absolutely whenever you hand over money – get a receipt. Insist, stand there until you get one, but get a receipt. Otherwise the Spanish game commences.

SKY TV

The one thing that Brits will not give up is their British

TV. BBC1, BBC2, ITV, Channel 4 and Channel 5 are a must. Some people have the full Sky package but many are happy to just have the basic channels in order to keep up to date with the news and soaps. Wait until it rains! In order to receive a signal in Spain you require a huge satellite dish. It makes me laugh sometimes when you visit someone's apartment and their satellite dish takes up half of their balcony – great view eh! Most of the year the weather on the Costa del Sol is fantastic and many people spend most of their spare time either round the pool, on the beach or on their balcony (if there's room). During the winter however, during a cold spell, people will light their gas bottle in a tin box and settle back to watch the news or corrie. Ah this is great. Then it starts to rain and due to the size of the stupid dishes the picture goes off.

Channel 5 is probably my favorite channel overall and guess which channel always goes off first, you've got it, Channel 5. It doesn't even have to rain for Channel 5 to go off, just a few clouds will do it. Sat there enjoying a documentary, and then all of a sudden the picture starts breaking up and the people start talking like Elmer Fudd.

The time when you most want to watch the TV you can't – great!

THE TRIP SWITCH

Ask them, anybody who has spent any reasonable amount of time in Spain. (The Trip Switch), it drives people to suicide, what's wrong with Spanish electricians?

With very few exceptions there can't be enough electrical power going into Spanish properties – can there? Is it the Brits who use more appliances than the Spanish, if so why? I can't understand it.

Every property we have lived in with the exception of one (it must have been near a power station), has had this bloody infuriating problem. You put the kettle on, fine. You then put a slice of bread in the toaster, fine – hopefully. Your wife then turns the iron or her hair dryer on and CLICK, there it goes, the trip switch in the electricity junction box. It appears that any two electrical appliances are the maximum you are allowed to use. CLICK, CLICK BLOODY CLICK, all the time. Most properties have worn out marble tiles directly in front of the junction box because that's where people spend most of their time. If you have a tumble drier or washing machine turned on then you may as well just go and sit on a stool at the bloody junction box for the full duration. Most have a door covering the actual trip switches and I can almost guarantee that if you look at a property which isn't brand new, then the junction box door will be either bent or completely broken. That's because most men spend half of their lives whacking the bastard thing out of sheer frustration. It should be an Olympic sport as us ex pats would win gold every time. Uuuuurrrrrrrgh!!!!!!!!

SOLAR PANELS

Where are they? What's wrong with this place, it's the

biggest asset they have. The sun is up there in the sky most of the day and most of the time. When the sun isn't there, it is never far away and yet you could spend all day driving around the Costa del Sol and would be lucky to see two solar panels. In the UK you can see solar panels on council houses in Leeds in the fog. It isn't logical!

I have asked Spanish people on numerous occasions, why don't you have solar heating? They just shrug and say 'I don't know.' I have already mentioned the fact that most properties are damp in the winter and solar panels would sort this out. Once you have paid for the installation then it's all free from the old currant bun. It may be that companies have tried to sell solar heating in southern Spain but they haven't made a very good job of it. Did they price them wrongly, I don't know. I cannot believe there isn't a British entrepreneur out there who could rustle up a few good salesmen and start whacking them in. A great opportunity awaits someone!

EL BANDITOS

Crime does not appear to be a massive problem on the Costa del Sol, or at least not from my personal experience. It is there though, and it comes in various guises. On the Costa del Sol we have –

The opportunists – These are the people who in summer 'sus' out who is sitting on the terrace of a bar or café. They work in two's, and if there is someone sat there with a juicy looking bag or a camcorder they will come in and sit on the next table. They usually just order a coffee or a soft drink and do one of two things. They will either sit there until the people on the next table are preoccupied and then leg it with the bag or camcorder, or they will operate (the blag). The favorite is to get a large paper map out and one of them will ask the people on the next table if they know where 'so and so' is. While they are doing this with the map unfolding in front of these poor peoples faces, the other one is dipping the bag or pocketing the camcorder.

The gypsy flower selling dippers – Now these people are cynical. They prey on the elderly and don't give a damn that in most cases they ruin peoples holidays and at worst, could give some of these poor victims a heart attack. They are women, and usually operate in two's or three's. One of these women will walk up to an elderly person and push a bunch of flowers or herbs in front of the unsuspecting persons face completely blocking their view. Whilst the flowers or herbs are half way up the persons nose the other hand will be dipping the bag. They are good, very good. I lost count of the number of times an old lady would come into our tea shop and tell us that she had been robbed by one of these people. Purse, passport, everything!

The Moroccan looking guys – If you ask anyone on the Costa del Sol who they believe commit the majority of crimes then most will say the 'Moroccan looking guys.' They are the opportunists, the people who smash car windows to steal something on the seat, the burglars and

LIFE'S A LAUGH ON THE COSTA—HONEST!

the late night muggers. I have only had one encounter with these guys and looking back I guess I could have finished up in hospital, but I hate people who rob me. One morning after putting out the tables and chairs on our terrace, I nipped round the corner to the local bakery which I did every morning. As I returned and came round the corner these two Moroccan looking guys were crossing our terrace laughing and had obviously just come out of our tea shop. I went in and asked Chris, what did those two want? As she had been in the kitchen, she hadn't seen anyone but said, 'where are our cigarettes, they were on the bar?' Never mind the cigarettes, where's my lighter? My son, Oliver, had bought me a Ted Baker Zippo lighter for my birthday and it meant a lot to me. It wasn't the cost, it was personal. These two tossers had just walked in, seen there was nobody around, nicked the cigarettes and lighter, then just walked out again laughing. A rush of steam and I legged it after these two guys. I caught up with them fairly quickly which wasn't easy in a pair of flip flops. I stuck my hand out and asked for the cigarettes and lighter back. The old (two onto one move slipped into gear) as the one on the left took a step to the side so there was now one of them directly in front of me and one to my left. Here we go, I've been here before, albeit many years ago. As it happened, he hadn't pushed the Lambert and Butler packet down into his pocket and the packet top was visible. I slipped off my flip flops one at a time slowly, took a step backwards, and pointed to the packet in his pocket – give them back. Now most of these guys carry knives so they must have thought I was either a lunatic or a karate expert (or both). The guy in front of me took the cigarettes out of his pocket and handed them to me. If they were going to make a move then it would come now, it didn't. I insisted he gave me the lighter back which he also did. Thieving bastards I said, and walked off trying to look hard but breathing ferociously.

It was probably a stupid thing to do and I could have come to grief, but why should you just let someone walk into your premises, take your property, and then let them go.

This is a classic – A Dutch friend of ours called Jacob who lives near our tea shop, kept having a read of parts of this book whilst I was writing it and giving me his opinion. He has lived in Spain for many years, speaks perfect Spanish, reads the Spanish newspapers and gets Spanish books from the library. One day he said, 'there is a book by a Spaniard which goes into Spanish scams, thefts and swindles. It includes one section on a man who managed to sell a whole Spanish village which didn't belong to him to a property developer. You would like it and may find it useful for your own book. I will go to the library, get it out and then translate the parts of interest into English.' Thanks that would be great. This guy came back to me a couple of days later with a grin on his face from ear to ear – 'I went to the library yesterday and the book has been nicked. It is on their computer as being in

LIFE'S A LAUGH ON THE COSTA—HONEST!

stock but it isn't there—someone has nicked it!'

Someone had stolen a book on stealing!

THE LANGUAGE

One thing we Brits are incredibly guilty of is not being bothered to learn the language. People can say whatever they want but in the cold light of day it comes down to one thing, PURE LAZINESS! How arrogant can you get? You come to live in a foreign country, cannot be bothered to learn the language, and then you are actually disappointed if you try to communicate with a local and they don't speak English. The problem down here is that there are probably too many Brits. If you went to live inland at a small village then you would have no choice but to learn the language. If you didn't speak Spanish, then not only would you not get anything done but you wouldn't stand a chance of being accepted.

There are so many Brits on the Costa del Sol that in reality you don't have to be able to speak Spanish. Whatever you want there is a Brit who supplies it. Many Spanish are all too aware of how important the British money is to their lives and jobs. Some may not admit it, but the Spanish know that they need the Brits just as much as the Brits need the Spanish. I believe the reason why there is so little resentment towards us invaders is the fact that they know we bring our own money into their country and claim very little back, if anything. Okay, we use their schools and hospitals but most pay National Insurance, are legally within the system, and pay their way.

There are lots of retail businesses which are owned by Brits. Everything from butchers to furniture shops to double glazing. You name it, and there is at least one British company supplying it. Many of the major Spanish outlets go out of their way to recruit sales staff who can speak English. If you go into one of the huge furniture retailers or DIY outlets you will almost always find at least one member of staff who speaks perfect English and signs in the shop will be in both Spanish and English. All of this combined means that the Brits don't have to speak Spanish. It shouldn't be the case, but that's the way it is. We know lots of people who started out with good intentions and began taking Spanish lessons. You can guarantee that within a few weeks at most they will have jacked it in. Whatever the reason, you could have taken bets on it, they sack it. If you are one of the majority who don't take Spanish lessons then you invariably pick it up as you go along. An odd word here, another one there, you see words on advertising posters etc. I take my hat off to anyone who has a go at the language. Start off slowly by going into a shop and instead of pointing or asking for something in English – have a go! Don't be afraid to get it wrong as the Spanish are usually very pleased that you are trying. Be careful though. As with any language there are some words which are similar to others but have completely different meanings. Some are embarrassing if you get them wrong –

For instance there is Huevos 'pronounced webbos' meaning eggs. On the other hand Jueves 'pronounced webbes,' means Thursday. If you are not careful you can ask for 'half a dozen Thursdays,' or indeed say to a friend, 'I'll meet you at seven o'clock on eggs' – eh!

Then there is the Spanish word for a box or crate which is Caja 'pronounced Caca.' On the other hand, the word Kaka means the same as it does in certain parts of the UK. Here again you could innocently get this completely wrong by asking a supplier for 'a crate of shit,' or say something like 'my dog has just had a box down the street.'

Chris's daughter can now speak fluent Spanish but a couple of years ago she went to a supermarket meat counter for a chicken and asked for some 'dick.' Chicken in Spanish is 'pollo' – pronounced 'poyo.' On the other hand the pronouncement 'poya' means 'dick, knob,' call it what you want but you get the message. 'Could I have some dick please,' not a good introduction to trying out your language skills with seven or eight elderly Spanish ladies standing behind you. She stopped going into that shop for some reason!

Also be careful if you say 'American' to a Spaniard. 'American,' if said quickly, can sound like 'Maricon' which in Spanish means 'puff' – 'Hello, are you a puff?' – oops!

If in doubt – gesticulate. That can be confusing too.

I don't know if it's a good thing or a bad thing, but I have never been afraid of making a fool of myself if I want something. If you don't speak the language and the person you are trying to communicate with doesn't speak English then gesticulate, why not. When we first arrived in Spain I often did this and yes, I did make a fool of myself. These are a couple of examples which I still remember –

I went into a fish mongers one day and wanted two swordfish steaks. I didn't have half a clue what swordfish was in Spanish so I said pescado, which is the plural of fish i.e. fishes. (You will have to use your imagination on this one). I then proceeded to raise my right arm and stick it out in front of my nose like a lop sided Nazi salute trying to resemble a swordfish. The woman looked at me as though I had just escaped from somewhere and called two guys in from the store room at the back of the shop. Off I go again, doing the swordfish impersonation and walking round the shop. By this time a couple of locals had come into the shop and they too looked at me in disbelief as I am quite carried away by now.

Pause, 'ah elephant' one of the guys said. What – I'd never thought of that, they thought I wanted some elephant. They were nodding their heads as though they were telling me that they didn't sell elephant. I just shrugged my shoulders, said gracias and walked out – what a tosser!

A similar thing happened just days after we arrived down here and I didn't even speak one word of Spanish. We were in a mini market in a small village so the English was none existent. I wanted some eggs but as far as the lady behind the counter was concerned, I could have been asking for an aircraft carrier. There I go, bent legs, arms bent with hands on hips doing a chicken impression and then stopping very quickly and dropping my arse lower as if laying an egg—ah, huevos! I got the eggs, it worked that time.

COWBOYS AND CON MEN

There are cowboys and con men on the Costa del Sol falling over themselves to rob you. There are electricians who are not really electricians, plumbers who are not really plumbers, refrigeration engineers who are really ex brickies, you name the profession and there are stacks of Brits claiming to be just that. In many cases these people are not qualified in anything but just fell into it by either working as a helper to a proper craftsman or they are self taught. Don't get me wrong, there are some extremely good qualified people here but for every one of those, there are ten cowboys.

One day when we were in our tea shop, the washing up water would not go down the plug hole. It's not surprising that this happens every now and again as bits of lettuce, baked beans and all sorts of stuff gets down there. Also in Spain for some reason, they never appear to have a natural fall on waste pipes. They run more or less horizontally—why is that, it's not logical? I did the usual, nipped round to the local hundred peseta shop (the local Arkwrights), and bought a new plunger. That didn't work so I then borrowed a drain rod wire from a friend but that didn't work either. Obviously if we cannot wash up then the business grinds to a halt so we had to close until the problem was sorted out. The building in which our business was housed is quite old and the (El Presidente) of the block liked everyone to use the same Spanish plumber for all work carried out. He knew the horizontal pipe layout and all the little quirks of the place. Fine. As it happened this plumber was in the building at the time as it appears there is always something for him to do. He has nearly a full time job in that one apartment block; he makes more or less a full time living out of it. He appeared about an hour later and proceeded to do everything I had already tried despite the fact that I had told him the proceedings to date. Surprise surprise, he couldn't shift the blockage either. As it was one of the many Spanish saint's days a couple of days later he said he would be back with some more equipment to fix it **'in about ten days time.'** Pardon, did I hear that right, yes, ten days time! That's okay then; we will close for ten days until you can get back at your leisure five weeks on Thrumsday. I don't think so. Bollocks to El Presidente.

I fell for it, Christ did I!

There are companies over here who call themselves by the same name as reputable companies in the UK even though they have no association with them whatsoever. Looking through the local English newspaper under (services), I noticed a drain company who had the same name as a very famous British drain unblocking company.

I was not wise to the way things are at that time so I wrongly assumed that this must be some kind of franchise. I called the number which was a mobile (I now know this is a giveaway as if they have no land line then they have no office, and if they have no office, then they are a one man band). Sure enough the guy turned up first thing the very next day and hopefully we could be back in business by the afternoon. I told him what action had been taken to date and he said he would have to get something out of his van. He then reappeared with this huge vacuum plunger thing, disconnected the pipes from the sinks and dishwasher exposing the pipe which went directly into the kitchen wall and down beneath the floor. He pumped this thing over and over and I could tell by the resistance that this was some blockage – then – whoosh – blockage gone and water flowed freely down the pipe. He reconnected the pipes; put more water down in order to prove the point, and I paid him eighty euros for his fifteen minutes work. It was well worth it as the blockage was clear now wasn't it – er – sort of! Not fifteen minutes later the janitor and El Presidente came running into our shop shouting and throwing their arms around like a couple of mental patients. Calm down, calm down. I thought they were trying to kidnap me as they were dragging me outside so I decided to just go with the flow and go wherever it was that they were trying to take me. Round the corner, through the underground garage door, turn the lights on, down the ramp and into the garage. There it was,

El Presidente's new Renault Cleo absolutely covered in thick slimy gungy shite, a shed load of it, and a pipe hanging down sadly through the plaster board ceiling. Mr. Vacuum-Pumper had cleared the blockage alright. He had blown the bloody pipe apart and far from all the crap flowing out into the sewerage system it had dropped onto El Presidente's car. What do you say – 'er – sorry!' I don't think El Presidente ever felt the same about that car. It's a good job it wasn't a rag top! That cost us the eighty euros for Mr. Vacuum-Pumper plus a serious car wash, plus another plumber to re-connect the pipe, plus a guy to re plaster the garage roof. Not a good investment!

The Spanish also have their own brand of con men in the form of bogus gas mechanics. They will walk into your business or come to the door of your home dressed in overalls which are the same colours as the major bottled gas supplier. Most Brits are fairly frightened of a Spaniard who looks official and speaks no English. These guys gesticulate in such a way as to make you understand that they wish to view your gas appliances. Once they view them, they then proceed to make a big issue of cutting the rubber pipe connecting the appliance to the gas bottle. 'Out of date, illegal.' They then put on a new length of rubber pipe, get you to sign a form and take eighty euros off you. You haven't a clue what you have signed, but actually it is a disclaimer saying that you have allowed them to rob you. The eighty euros can vary depending on how rich you look. Not bad work if you can get it as that length of pipe costs you pennies at the DIY shop. They have nothing whatsoever to do with the gas company in question and they make an absolute fortune out of this scam day after day. Stripe the Brits, they're easy money.

The other Spanish favorite is the (Fire Extinguisher) guy. They specialize in visiting bars which have recently changed hands. The new owner hasn't a clue about what's what so these guys march in and ask to see your fire extinguishers which you have to have by law. They will then shake their heads, lift the extinguishers out of their housings and take them away returning a couple of minutes later with new ones. 'You should have changed these before as they are out of date. One hundred and twenty euros please.' Now if the bar owner had looked at the labels on the fire extinguishers, he would have seen that they were not out of date at all. He would also see that this new guy was not even from the same company as highlighted on the labels of the original extinguishers. Striped again!

I sincerely hope that none of you will ever need an undertaker whilst on holiday over here. Beware if you do. We had as regular customers a lovely couple from Liverpool, Tony and Helen Stapleton. They came to Fuengirola regularly, Tony still does. They loved the place and were here so often, and for so long, that they knew just about all the Brits in Western Fuengirola. They were looked upon as locals. Unfortunately Helen died whilst over here during July 2005. She was a lovely lady whom

Tony idolized. Tony woke up during one night to find that Helen wasn't beside him as normal so he went into the hall and Helen had unfortunately already passed away. She was lying on the hall floor. Tony alerted the police and they, in turn, called an undertaker. Not a lot of sympathy from this guy. The first words he spoke to Tony were 'if you want to take her back to England it will cost you 6,000 euros.' Poor Helen was still on the floor, can you believe that! Things took their course at the undertakers until the company in question contacted Tony again informing him that there was a shortfall in the insurance. Tony would have to find a further 1,730 Euros in cash, immediately; otherwise they would not release Helen. He coughed up, he would wouldn't he! As things became clear, it transpired that the undertaker had placed Helen in his most expensive coffin. No asking which coffin Tony would like or 'did he have a budget.' In circumstances like that the last thing you are going to argue about is the money it is costing for your wife's coffin. The undertaker was obviously banking on that. Is anyone really going to turn around and say, 'well that coffin is too expensive so you had better take her out and put her in a cheaper one.' To make matters far worse, a coffin for transport back to the UK has to be metal lined making it completely useless for cremation. The life of the coffin was a few days until the UK undertaker could transpose coffins, and the Spanish undertaker must have known that. How cynical can you get? In order to illustrate just how mercenary this guy was, he then contacted the owner of the apartment that Tony and Helen had been renting. The undertaker told him that if anyone else ever died in one of his properties then a phone call to him with the custom would secure 500 euros a time – what a complete blood sucker!

On a brighter note, everyone rallied round Tony and made things as good as they could for him in order to cope with the loss of (his pal). That's what he called her. The local Brits chipped in and sent over to Liverpool a beautiful wreath for the funeral. There is a plant outside the Lounge Bar in Fuengirola which the owners, Pete and Garry have tried to kill on numerous occasions as they didn't like it for some reason. They have tried to pull it up, ripped pieces off it and even poured bleach over it. Everyone thought it was dead. Early the very same evening that she passed away, Helen walked over to the plant, watered it and pulled the dead leaves off saying that it was a shame, and that it would come back. Chris and I were there having a drink with them at the time, we saw it. I swear to God that within a week of Helen passing away that plant sprang into life and it is now a complete picture of health. We all now call that plant Helen, and won't let anyone near it.

BRITISH BARS

There are many excellent British bars along the Costa del Sol, everything anyone could ever want. There are sports bars, Irish theme pubs, betting bars, jazz bars, blues and soul bars, the lot. I am sorry to say however, that some of the British owned bars are complete dustbins owned and run by people who either can't be bothered or genuinely haven't got a clue. They are a disgrace and make a massive contribution to giving the Brits a bad name. At least in the UK the major pub chains operate a training programme for new staff and hopefully if they are completely useless then they are out. You can go into literally hundreds of bars over here and the bar and tables will be permanently sticky, the spirit bottles on the shelves full of dust, mirrors within which you cannot see yourself and toilets where you would not send your dog. Why, it shouldn't be so. Most of the time these bar owners have absolutely nothing to do because hardly anyone goes in. Why don't they clean? They have thrown the towel in and just lean on the bar reading a newspaper with a self filling pint in front of them. Sometimes these bar owners are so pissed, so often, that they will pay some unfortunate person a pittance to look after their bar for a few hours a day while they sleep it off.

We got to know a guy who is deaf and his speech is bad due to this. He can lip read perfectly. He was desperate for a job as he had come over with a limited amount of money and was at desperation point to generate some cash. He started frequenting a particular bar and the locals thought he was great. Now, a deaf bar man is not a common sight anywhere, but the owners of this bar offered him a job for just a couple of hours a day so they could have a siesta. He was elated. What they were paying him was really taking the mickey but due to his circumstances he was happy to have the job at least until something better came along. This guy came into a pub we were in after he had been working for a few days and was laughing his head off. He couldn't wait to tell us what had happened earlier in the day and wasn't afraid to laugh at himself. Apparently he had been behind the bar in the pub and there were no customers in. A couple of regular customers appeared outside and were waving at him so being polite, he waved back. He was telling us between fits of laughter that these people then reappeared and were waving again. He waved back again. Then another guy appeared and he started waving his arms around also. Our friend waved back. This went on for more than a few minutes when the owner suddenly appeared and was fuming. He ran past our friend, grabbed some step ladders and stretched up to the fire alarm on the wall. Those people had been waving at our friend trying to tell him that the alarm was ringing like hell and '***was there a fire?***' Of course he couldn't hear it – he's deaf. It's a good job there wasn't a real fire! After two weeks the bar owners sacked our friend for no reason and to this day he hasn't been paid a cent. Great Brits eh! Then there are the bar owners who quite literally take the piss. It would not be allowed in the UK, but there are bars which increase their prices by the clock. There is a large pub on the sea front in Fuengirola where Chris and

I went for a drink one afternoon shortly after we arrived in Spain. It was around 5.30 p.m. and I bought a pint of lager and a small shandy for Chris. Four euros eighty, a bit pricey but not too bad. We sat on the terrace in the sun and enjoyed our drink. 'Shall we have another – why not.' I went back to the bar and ordered the same drinks. The bar man asked me for another one euro and fifty cents. But I have just had these same drinks and paid four euros eighty cents. 'Yes but we increase our prices at 6.00 p.m., again at 9.00 p.m. and then again at midnight.' Not with me you don't pal – you can stick them where the sun don't shine. We walked out and never went back.

TOWN DRIVING

The discipline is just not there when it comes to driving in Spain. Indicators, what are those? It appears that when you buy a new car in Spain then indicators must come as extras. Even when they are used by the driver in front, it's a fifty fifty chance whether they are using the correct one. On the odd occasion you do see the car in front indicating, then there is no way you would believe the signal. Indicate left, turn right, indicate right, turn left – it's simple really. You can be driving down a street in town when the car in front of you just stops for no apparent reason. The driver will get out and go into the bakery for a loaf of bread. There isn't enough room to go round him so you just wait until he comes out, gets back in his car and drives on. You do get used to it eventually, honest! At first you sit there blasting your horn and the guy just looks at you as if you are mental so what's the point, stay loose, and calm down, this is Spain. If it happened in the UK people would be fighting in lumps. Stopping to get a loaf of bread and expecting other motorists to just sit there and wait, I don't think so. You would finish up with a baguette shoved up your arse–sideways!

SYNCHRONIZED TRAFFIC LIGHTS, WHAT ARE THEY?

You can drive along virtually any road in any town along the Costa del Sol and, as in the UK; there will be a set of traffic lights at every junction. The difference is that rather than being synchronized so that there is traffic flow, and by the time you get to the next set they are at green, it's the other way around. Do they do it on purpose, just for a laugh? There is no point in having more than two gears in your car when you are driving in town. You get used to it and just take it for granted after a while. The lights change, you take twenty seconds to put the car in gear and then crawl to the next set, there's no rush. The Spaniards have always lived here so you would think they would get used to it as well–no! There he is, at the side of you, Pedro Schumacher in a completely illegal 1970's Seat Ibiza–he's off. You then have to go even slower as you can't see where you are going for all the smoke coming out of this heap of junk. You would be quicker having someone walking in front of you with a red flag!

WHO ATE ALL THE CAR ROOF AERIALS

Wherever you go on the Costa del Sol, you will notice that virtually every car which should have a roof aerial hasn't got one. Where do they all go, it's a total mystery. Chris and I must have bought five replacements within our first six months here. If someone nicks a roof aerial, and that person in turn nicks someone else's roof aerial and so on, then these objects would just travel around from car to car, wouldn't they? Apparently not. Someone must just walk round all day, every day, nicking roof aerials and then either eating them or burning them. Where do they all go?

WALKING ON 'NUT' SHELLS

Why is it that lots of Spaniards think they are budgies?

We used to arrive at our tea shop regularly and we could always tell if a Spaniard had been stood on our terrace the previous evening watching the world walk by. There were nut shells all over the place. They stand there with a bag full of these things, taking the tiny nuts out of the shells and then dropping the shells around their sandals.

If there were a few of them, we finished up with what resembled a full aviary!

SCOOTERS

The one thing which does need sorting out is the scooter driver. The kids who drive these scooters are serious suicide cases and some of them do not look to be any more than thirteen or fourteen years old. They cut you up, overtake on the inside, do wheelies on the seafront whilst overtaking, and drive on the pavements. It is not uncommon to see them driving a scooter whilst speaking into a mobile telephone and smoking a cigarette, all at the same time. Many of the scooters are obviously not roadworthy, they are complete wrecks and hardly anyone wears a crash helmet. I thought Spain was in the EEC but the police turn a complete blind eye to the lack of crash helmets. It is not only the youngsters who are dicing with theirs and others lives. You will often see a man on a large motorbike or scooter driving along with no crash helmet and a toddler sat in front of him also with no head protection. If they ran into something or came off, then it doesn't bear thinking about.

The police in southern Spain really do need to start acting tough with these people. It's not as if they don't see it happening. During the summer of 2004, Chris and I were walking through Fuengirola when all of a sudden a number of police on motorbikes and police cars came down the road with horns blowing and blue lights flashing. They blocked the junction where we were standing and all the traffic ground to a halt. Something was happening and it had a police escort. We waited a couple of minutes and then this seemingly never ending stream of motorcycles came through. It was a massive motorcycle rally and most were beautiful Harley Davidson's. Bearing in mind the police are there waving these bikes through each junction, plus there were police motorcycle escorts at either side of the rally; most of the riders didn't have crash helmets on. Worse still, some of them had very young children with them either straddling the petrol tank or just sat there in front of their (presumably) fathers. Some were three or four years old and the police were completely oblivious to it – astonishing.

In the UK you would be lucky to get fifty yards.

PEOPLE WHO HAVE GLASS CURTAINS

Double glazing, UPVC windows, call them what you want, the aesthetics and fit in Spain are way behind the UK standard generally. However, they do have these things call (glass curtains). Because most people live in apartments on the Costa del Sol and because it can get quite cold during the winter months, many people put glass curtains around their balcony in order to gain an extra room. They look fantastic, well that's probably not the best way to describe them as you can hardly see them. They are sheet glass panels about half a metre wide with no frame, stretching from the top of the balcony to the floor. They fold back when it is warm and they are brilliant, they look classy and they are extremely functional – BUT! There are people over here who appear to spend all day, every day, cleaning the bloody things. That amount of sheet glass takes some cleaning and even when they are clean, they are not really clean. Stand back and admire your work, there's always another bit that's got a mark on it. You can spot them on your urbanization; they always have a window blade in their hand or a squeegee. They might live on the top floor but there they are, round the pool, looking up at their balcony with a blade in their hand. They shake their head, leg it back upstairs, blade it again and then reappear round the pool a few minutes later with that bloody window blade in their hand again.

What's wrong with them, kick the glass out, sit in the open air, get a beer, play cards, it's not worth it!

SPANISH COMPANIES AND TRADESMEN

I have touched on this one before when we required a plumber to unblock a drain in our tea shop. I know for a cast iron fact that many Brits living in Spain would love to use Spanish companies or tradesmen if they could. The fact is that they are, generally speaking, totally unreliable. Punctuality and rushing is something that is completely alien to them. It's the culture (I think) and it will probably take them ten or twenty years more to wake up to the fact that Brits don't like to wait, they want it now. They will pay for it, but they want it now. How these people are missing out. It's not a language thing as pointing to a water leak or a blown out circuit board is not difficult. Brits will pay for a good quick job and from my experience they would be more than happy to use Spaniards if they could rely on them, in fact they would like to use them. It's a terrible shame but you will try it, be more than disappointed and go back to 'Fred, I'm a qualified plumber – honest!' What a shame, it shouldn't be like that.

IF BEING ANNOYED OCCASIONALLY IS THE PAY BACK FOR THIS GREAT LIFE STYLE, THEN LET'S BE ANNOYED!

CHAPTER EIGHT

The lifestyle

I guess there must be people who do not particularly like the sun, but if you do, then what a place this is to live. They reckon the Costa del Sol gets on average three hundred and thirty days of sunshine per year. That means that you can actually plan to have a barbeque two weeks on Saturday and can almost guarantee that you will be in the garden or on the roof in the glorious sunshine having a fantastic time. In the UK you would plan the same thing, invite some friends round, buy in the necessaries, and then finish up cooking it in the garage. You pretend that you are enjoying yourself, we've all done it. What's the bloody point? You live inside in the UK and that is the main difference to living over here. For most of the year, we live outside. If you live in an apartment then the place which gets the most use is the balcony. You will sit out there first thing in the morning with a cup of tea or coffee prior to going to work (if you work), then you will sit out there in the evening to eat your meal. Inevitably you will also sit out there on your days off. People will often spend more money on balcony furniture than they do on their lounge suit, it's fantastic. The bigger the balcony the better, and if you have a direct sea view then you have got the lot. It's as good as it gets!

SEE THE 'REAL' SPAIN

All too often the Brits who live over here never get to see the real Spain, the Costa del Sol isn't the real Spain. I have lost count of the number of times I have heard people down here say things like, 'I'm sick of this place,' or 'I'm bored.' Okay, get off your arse and do something about it then. You have to make the effort and drive inland in order to explore the real culture of the place, it's there so don't miss it. We are lucky on the Costa del Sol as a couple of hours driving at most will take you to some fantastic places. For me one of the nicest places you can visit from here is actually also one of the nearest, Mijas Pueblo. (Pueblo) means village and that's just what Mijas is. Although the place has changed in terms of now having numerous souvenir shops, restaurants and bars, you still get the Spanish village feel. As you enter Mijas Pueblo there is a massive multi storey car park so finding somewhere to leave the car is not a problem and there is also an excellent regular bus service from Fuengirola. There are three main levels to Mijas and everywhere you go you will spot another tiny little street or a set of steps leading to somewhere or other. Don't get a guide book, just wander. There are fantastic cafes, bars and restaurants. Some of these are actually built into the cliffs and the views are stunning, you look down on Fuengirola and it looks like a model village. Children love it too as there are donkeys which are available for hire for a modest cost. Go there!

It is difficult to believe, but as you are sat on the sea front in Benalmadena or Fuengirola during the winter months, often with sunshine and a mid to top sixties temperature, you can see snow on the distant mountains of the Sierra Nevada. You can drive from brilliant sunshine to the ski resort in less than two hours, amazing. The last time we went up there we set off in the hairdresser's car dressed in shorts and tea shirts. We stopped in a lay by half way up the mountain and changed into jeans and a sweater. Once we arrived at the ski village we donned boots, another sweater, Chris a sheep skin coat, and me a thick over coat, it was minus five degrees. We took Dino with us and he had obviously forgotten what a British winter feels like as he was walking on the snow as if it was broken glass, shivering and generally being a pain in the arse. A walk around, a cup of coffee, (I wish they had Bovril), and back to the car, sod that. If you like skiing then it must be great but we don't so back to the coast we went – quickly! Instead of going back the way we came through Granada, we dropped straight back to the coast near Nirja and within an hour we had stopped to put our shorts back on. The contrast in temperature is unbelievable; you have got it all, from sunshine to skiing in an hour or so.

We once decided that we wanted a few days break from the tea shop so we took advantage of having our own business, we shut! It was a spur of the moment thing during February and I phoned the kennels to book Dino in. We set off early the following morning on a three day adventure and we took the donkey route (really crap road) to Rhonda which cuts through the hills and mountains from Coin (pronounced Cohen). This is a fantastic drive but much easier if you happen to be driving a half track. You drive through stretches of countryside which are typically Spanish and other areas which resemble Scotland or the Lake District, absolutely beautiful. Being out of season we had no problem booking into a hotel in Rhonda right next to the gorge which splits the town in half. We wandered around the town for the day, went to a Spanish restaurant for the menu del dia (menu of the day), a couple of drinks, and then back to the hotel, 'this is proper Spain' we said. We got up the following morning and then drove to Seville. In many ways Seville is like most Cities around the world insofar as it has had bits added on to it over the years but we wanted to stay in a hotel near the Cathedral, in the original old city. No problem again with accommodation, two star only but virtually new and very clean with en suite and right in the centre of the original City. We checked in, had a quick shower and then went out for a walk. Similar to London there are buses which go around the City passing numerous sights and buildings of interest. You can pick these buses up at various points around the City and then get off to catch another one which takes in a different route. This enables you to see something else you might be interested in. We walked to the nearest pick up point for a tourist bus and were amused by the fact that these buses were actually old London buses. They were open top, right hand drive London buses, how strange. It was quite cold so the coats were on again. Sods law I guess, but we had no sooner got onto the bus when the heavens opened and when it rains in Spain it rains, it rains a lot. Here we are on an open top bus and we couldn't have got any wetter if we had walked into the sea fully clothed (I think I did that once). There weren't many people on the bus, the standard issue Japanese tourists with ten cameras around their necks, and American tourists talking at the top of their voices because they think they are interesting, plus a few Brits—on the top deck with us. When it started to rain everyone except the Brits disappeared to the ground floor but not us lot, we were about as pissed wet through as it is possible to get so what's the point, we are here for the views and the views we will get. We switched routes and changed buses a couple of times. In total we drove around on the top deck of various buses for a good two to three hours. When we eventually got off we stepped straight into the street which was, no exaggeration, about four inches deep in water, it was a river. My cromby must have weighed about two hundredweight. If I had spent ten minutes under a power shower I could not have been wetter and our feet were squelching big style. The Spaniards were looking at us as though we were mental patients as we were laughing our heads off, it was beyond a joke but we thought it was hilarious. We were armed with a street plan so we guessed from our drop off point that we were about fifteen to twenty minutes walk from our hotel. To do that walk, in that weather, was virtually impossible. Head for the Cathedral and try to find a café, instead we found a pub – big mistake! 'I'll have a pint.' That was it. We stayed there, out of the rain, until we had downed about eleventeen beers and being the strong Spanish stuff we walked back out into the rain like a couple of hermit crabs. We got back to our hotel eventually, looking like something out of a horror film. Squelchy shoes, water dripping off our hair and coats, giggling, walking sideways with rubber legs and trying to ask the nice lady receptionist for the key in Spanglaise which we thought was funny but she obviously didn't. We didn't see the evening as we thought we should have a Siesta and didn't wake up until the following morning. When we did wake up, it was as if we were living in a gypsy camp. There were clothes spread all over the floor, hanging off the wardrobe, over the shower rail, 'has it been raining clothes?' Obviously in a state of complete twattiness we had laid our clothes out to dry, 'did we do that, huh, I can't remember, can you?' 'Shut up I've got a headache.' Anyway, embarrassed at breakfast we then paid the bill, 'did we drink all that from the mini bar as well?' Everyone goes (on one) occasionally.

We think it's nice in Seville, but we can't quit remember!

Back to sensible mode. We drove out of Seville and wanted to go through the lakes back to Fuengirola so we headed off the main motorway towards the lakes. Beautiful scenery again, the rain had stopped so we could have been driving through Scotland but with sun. We stopped a few times to take in the views and then went to a restaurant in El Chorro which is elevated and overlooking one of the lakes. Menu del Dia again and 'look at that view – that's the real Spain.' Three days of wonderment apart from the lost evening in Seville.

There is Granada, Seville, Cordoba, lots and lots of places to visit and appreciate. Fuengirola, Benalmadena, Nirja, Marbella and Puerta Banus are great for the tourist run but see the rest, it's the best! It is far too easy to slip into the same old thing and not see anything.

SPANISH RESTAURANTS

'I don't like that foreign food' – well piss off to Blackpool then.

Spanish restaurants and ventas are marvellous. Shoot off into the hills and drop in at one of the thousands of ventas at the roadside in the brilliant sunshine. Enjoy a great meal for what you would pay for two pints on the coast. Don't feel frightened, they won't speak English but they will welcome you (in their own way). Swordfish, lamb cooked for so long that it falls apart as soon as you touch it, great local wine – relax! Well, try to relax. There will probably be a few Spanish families sat at tables around you shouting to the extent that you will think they are about to shoot each other but it's just a gentle conversation to them. Look at them, smile, put some ear plugs in, then enjoy your meal.

Do you really want to go to Smelly Melly's for burger and chips?

'GRACIAS, POR FAVOR' – IT'S NOT NECESSARY – IS IT?

It's a British thing and it's a nice British thing, it really is. Good manners, being polite, it's part of our history. I like it!

Please, thank you! – It costs nothing. That is the way it should be and it's the way that most of us have been brought up. Common courtesy, it means a lot, it tells people a lot about you. Common manners, they're simple and nice. Going back into the book I mentioned the fact that I got 'a smack around the back of the head' if I didn't say it. Fair enough – it didn't do me any harm – *I don't think so anyway?*

People come to Spain and sometimes think the Spanish serving them in shops and bars are ignorant because they don't get a 'por favor' or a 'gracias.' It's not necessary most of the time, it's a different culture. I couldn't get my head round it initially until we spoke one day to a Scottish lady who was married to a Spanish waiter. I can't remember how we got onto the subject, but she just laughed and said that her husband came in from the terrace on numerous occasions when she was waiting for him to finish his shift and said in Spanish, 'Christ, if those English people say "please" or "thank you" once more I swear that I will strangle the bastards. Why do they keep saying "please" and "thank you"—I'm sick of it—WHY DO THEY DO THAT—WHY?' You see, it annoys them when we do say it. It also annoys us when they do not say it. Who's right and whose wrong—nobody—it's the culture. Accept it. Please and thank you. It is not necessary all of the time in the Spanish culture, they are not being ignorant, it's just not necessary.

DRESS

Forget the long trousers, socks, shoes and even your shirt. For most of the year all these items of clothing are either hung up in the spare wardrobe or in a suitcase under the bed.

A pair of shorts and flip flops, that's standard issue. Dress is one of many things in Spain which is irrelevant in terms of status. You don't judge someone on the way they dress, how can you. You can hardly make a fashion statement at a barbeque with a pair of shorts and flip flops. Okay, you may have a designer logo on one or both but that means nothing anyway as you can buy rip off designer gear at the local market for a few euros. It's a great leveller because you may turn up wearing genuine, very expensive designer shorts, designer sandals and a Rolex watch, but I can say with a great deal of confidence that everyone else will assume that they are scammers from the local market or one of the many lookie lookie men. So why bother? The same goes for the ladies. There are of course certain ladies who will go the whole hogg. They dress completely unnecessarily over the top with a posh frock, gold shoes and gold handbag. Once at the party or barbeque you can watch them gradually looking more and more uncomfortable. A nice pair of sandals, a thin skirt and bikini top or a thin cotton dress, that's all you need and generally speaking that's the way it is. You save a fortune on clothes because you don't actually need many.

CARS

A new car, I don't think so!

There is another saying over here, 'never judge anyone by the car they drive.' The reason for this is that it is completely pointless having a decent car. Even if you do have one, it won't stay that way for very long. When we first got to Spain in our hairdressers Beetle there was not even a hairline scratch on it. After only a week or so we returned to the car and there was a bash on the corner of the rear colour coordinated bumper – oh hell, no, who's done that, what a bastard, I was distraught. Like most men, I have always taken great pride in our cars. I was the one on the drive every Sunday with the car wax, T-Cut, upholstery cleaner, the lot. A short while later there was another knock on the front bumper and at the end of our first year the car resembled the Bluesmobile, apart from the silly colour. In no time at all I was into the Spanish way, oh the car's been whacked again, shrug my shoulders, get in and then drive away.

The next time you are in Spain, look at the rear of cars. Tow bars, thousands of them – get one! It's a must accessory, far more useful than indicators. You can watch them park, it's a hobby. They reverse in and whack the car behind with their tow bar, pull forward and touch the car in front and then reverse into the centre of the space. Easy, parked, that's it, job done. We know some seriously rich people over here who drive cars with knocks all over them. It's not worth going and getting it fixed as you can put money on it that it will have been whacked again within a couple of weeks. Another saving you see. In the UK it is the done thing to change your car every two or three years and if it gets knocked it is straight into the garage for a re-spray. 'You can't be driving about in a car looking like that can you?'

There is no status symbol in a car over here!

I FANCY A DRINK

Now alcohol is a funny thing. It is part of our culture in Britain to go out and get as pissed as possible in as short a period of time as possible. Things have changed a little since the relaxation of pub opening hours but the culture is still alive. You work hard, so you play hard, especially Friday nights and weekends – I did! In Spain there has never been a problem getting a drink and it is much much cheaper here. As such the Spanish have never had to rush as much down their necks as possible. As often as not they will have a coffee and then enjoy a couple of glasses of wine with their evening meal.

You would be amazed at the places where you can get an alcoholic drink. For instance, shortly after we arrived in Fuengirola I took our Beetle to the local VW Garage for a service. As agreed, I went back to collect the car later in the day and it wasn't quit ready. Whilst waiting I noticed one of the mechanics coming out of the workshop to a vending machine in the office and buying a can. Out it rolled and I had to double take, it was a can of beer. They had a vending machine selling mineral water, soft drinks – and beer – in a garage! Can you imagine that in the UK. There would be mechanics falling all over the place, writing cars off by the dozen, 'your cars not ready yet, so what, do you want a fight?'

You can walk into a McDonalds in Spain and quite easily order a Big Mac and eleventeen beers. What more could you want.

This may sound an awful thing to say, but Brits who live over here quite like it when someone they know is taken into hospital; especially the Costa del Sol hospital in Marbella. The Brits are the most enthusiastic hospital visitors in Spain – why – because there is a cafeteria which is really a bar. A patient will wonder why their visitor appears to be irritable. 'Ooh, it's hot in here; I think I will just go for a wander around.' The patient doesn't see them again. If you walk into this cafeteria and look around, you can spot the Brits immediately. There will be Spanish families with a sandwich and coffee or a doughnut and a coke. You will then see tables littered with beer bottles – guess who? They're pissed up, full of sympathy – and beer! Can you imagine a hospital bar in the UK – just think about it – I don't think so do you?

The one secret heaven for many Brits over here is (The Petrol Station). Many of the petrol stations over here, particularly the large ones on major roads, have a bar attached to them and are open twenty four hours a day. That's right, you can drive in at four o'clock in the morning, fill up, and down six pints. It's dangerous you know! There is one of these petrol stations quite near our house. On the odd occasion we go out to a party or a club, we will get the taxi to drop us off at the petrol station for a night cap. There they are, it's three o'clock in the morning and the Brits are in. A table covered with empty pint glasses and car keys. Now remember that the beer over here is much stronger than that in the UK. A standard lager in the UK is about 4% whereas over here it is 5.5% – 5.6%. You can watch them, particularly if they are tourists in a hire car who are not aware of the beer strengths. They probably only came in for a quick pint when they noticed the bar whilst filling up. They then have another, and after four or five pints of this rocket fuel (the stare) arrives on their face. Before you know what's going on someone is saying to a poor Spaniard in the corner, 'hey you, did you just call my pint a puff?' Here we go again, I'll back you up until your nose bleeds – because – there lurks the unexpected. Unfortunately for some of these people, what they are not aware of is the fact that some of the best customers in these bars during the night are the police. Yes, that's right; it is not unusual to see police in the petrol station at 3.00 a.m. having a nice whiskey or six.

PREPARE FOR ALL 'YOUR MATES'

You find when you move to Spain that all of a sudden some people you knew (not particularly well) in the UK, miss you dreadfully. Family and close friends visit you and it's terrific to see them. Then there are the people who phone or e-mail telling you that 'it would be great to see you again and we were thinking of coming over for a week.' Yea right, pay for a cheap flight and get a free holiday. It's an amazing fact that when you say to these people, yes that would be great, I'll fish around and see what price I can get for an apartment for you to stay in. Inevitably the answer will be – 'oh, right, yes, of course.' They tend not to come then!

We have family and close friends over to visit regularly and in those circumstances it really is a pleasure to see them and have them staying with us. We have all got each others range now, but to start with everyone who visited us thought that we were on holiday as well. 'Where shall we go tonight then? Do you fancy a Chinese and then we could go to a bar where they have live entertainment. On Sunday we could shoot up into the mountains and have a meal at a nice little Spanish restaurant. Rhonda, we haven't been there, I've heard it's really nice, can we go there as well?' When you have to get up for work the following morning, the last thing you want to do is go to some music bar until daft o'clock and get completely pissed on loopy cocktails. If you are on holiday, fair enough, but we aren't. It didn't take us long to start telling visitors in the nicest possible way that it would be far easier and better if they hired a car in order for them to do their own thing some of the time. A couple of close friends of ours, Garry and Alison, come over two or three times a year with their little girl Lilly and we all get along great. As soon as they arrive we sit down (usually in a bar) and work out what we want to eat during their stay. Both Garry and I love cooking so the girls think it's great. We decide what we would like, say a Mexican one evening, a steak another evening, whatever. Garry and I then go to the supermarket (there's a bar there as well), buy all the gear we need for the week and split the bill. That's perfect and that's the way it should be. In the beginning we had people staying with us and they never dipped into their pockets once. They emptied the freezer and the bloody cupboards. We would work all day and then get home to a bowl full of washing up and then start cooking again whilst they were on a sun lounger on the balcony, great. I call that taking the piss.

Beware of the mates you forgot you had!

'NO WIN, NO FEE' – THAT'S A LAUGH!

It is unlikely that you will ever hear those words over here. Visit anywhere along the Costa del Sol and there is building work going on. Roads are constantly being dug up, pavements changed to accommodate parking bays, massive craters appearing which will eventually be underground car parks. You struggle to drive into Fuengirola two days running without some road or other being closed and the traffic diverted in another direction, usually the wrong one! Wherever you go there is something being dug up and the Spanish are far from organized when it comes to coning off or segregating areas where you can and cannot walk. It's very difficult for the older people in particular, but surprisingly enough the Spanish people just seem to take it in their stride and get on with it. In the UK there would be people falling over in droves armed with a camera and then getting straight on the blower for compensation. Over here things don't work like that. If you fall over then speak to the Town Hall or the police, you will get the same answer and that's the end of it – 'You should watch where you are going.'

That's fair enough; I don't have a problem with that.

POLITICAL CORRECTNESS

There has been a lot of publicity about racism in Spanish football and that can't be right. Overall however, political correctness is not something which exists in every day Spanish life. You can't say this, you can't do that, of course you can. The Spanish just do what they have always done. They are quite rightly proud of their history, proud of their traditions, and nobody is going to start telling them to change.

The one solitary example I saw of an attempt at political correctness had me in stitches. For years along the sea front in Fuengirola there were very large skip size plastic bins on wheels. Bar and restaurant owners would put their rubbish into these after a days work, ready for the bin men to empty during the night. As is the norm,' one day work men arrived opposite our tea shop and started digging a bloody great hole in the pavement. This hole got bigger and bigger. Eventually they lowered large metal bins into the holes which were on hydraulic elevators. They were to be new underground bins and the eye sore plastic skips could be taken away. This was a great move and would certainly improve the aesthetics of the promenade. Once all the bins and hydraulics were in place, they then put huge lids on them and three funnels came out of the lid. These were in effect chutes for the rubbish to go down into the relevant bin. Two were for any household and perishable waste, the other was for plastic material and cardboard. Now I have a great respect for blind people and in no way am I taking the mickey. Once the work was finished I went across and observed these new chutes and there, on each one, was a sign highlighting the type of rubbish you could put down them. Underneath the graphics was another large sticker in (brail). These chutes are actually sticking out of the pavement with no barrier or anything. The only way a blind person would know these chutes were there was when they fell over one. I guess they could then feel the sticker and know if they had fallen over the plastic chute or the household waste chute. Crazy!

NEWSPAPERS

Things have changed over recent years and you can now buy virtually any British newspaper on the same day whereas they were a day old going back a few years. The only difference is that you will pay at least two euros for it. On the Costa del Sol there are also numerous English speaking free papers and these include The SUR in English, The Town Crier, The Euro Weekly and The Friday Ad. Different papers come out on different days and generally speaking they are very good. The SUR in English is a must if you are looking for property or a job and The Town Crier is good for news. When I first arrived in Spain, I was fascinated by some of the adverts and what these papers were allowed to print. Under the heading (Adult Relaxation), there are two full pages in the edition which I have in front of me now. I am far from naïve, in fact I like to think that I have been a bit of a Jack the Lad in my time, but some things must have passed me by. Are they speaking in some kind of code, what does it mean, the mind boggles.

I highlight below a few of these ads, word for word, and letter for letter. How do they get away with it?

VERY attractive, tall, slim, clean, non smoking, brunette, 33 y.o. Hairy, shaven. Phone 000000000

'Which is it then, you can't be both – can you?'

PORN films. All original, latest titles. 'View before you buy.' Tel. Dave: 000000000. Free same day delivery. Malaga-Sotogrande.

Free same day delivery – 'view before you buy.' Does that mean that (Dave) watches them with you when he delivers?

FANCY a three some? Niki, big busted natural (40E) big body, voluptuous figure, excellent O levels plus much more. Mark, good looking, well built. Why not join us? Call Mark 000000000

What have the O levels got to do with it?

MARBELLA Jennifer, European, brunette, blue eyes, twenty-three, 1.78, nymphomania, 120-60-90. Bisexual, playful, seeks man, couples, French without, Greek, serious and discreet. 000000000

French without, I think I get that. What the hell is Greek?

SAN PEDRO Sexy–blonde–pretty woman, 100 boobs. Beautiful lingerie. Hotels, visits. 000000000

100 boobs–wow–now that's some woman.

NEW Thai good looking gay, specialist prostate stimulation, profesional thai body massage, by Appointment. Marbella 000000000

Aaaarrrrgh–Ouch, prostate stimulation–just reading it makes me get squiggles up my bum!

SHE MALE in Marbella, very femenine, sexy and hot attractive woman, speak perfect English. Nices big teats, fully functional. I can come big loads. Domination and cross dressing, I have the high thighs boots, wigs, leather, drinks, dildos, x rates movies, poppers, also slave female available. Begin ners and couples welcomed. 000000000

Doesn't read like perfect English to me but what is–Fully functional? Poppers?

GERMAN charming lady Eva, 40 Blonde, big bust 80DD. I like soft with lovely dessous and dirty games. 000000000

Soft with dessous–'what's that please'?

BIG BOOBED English blonde, sexy and flirty, loves fun, adorable looking, loves sucking cocks, dresses to please in lingerie stockings and heels, for hot sex and horny fun, Call Donna 000000000 Marbella.

No misunderstandings there then, I do like a straight talker!

MARRIED. "Educated Married" Consultation Doctors. Unforgettable Massage. Unforgettable Fantasies. 000000000

Consultant Doctors—surely you can get struck off for doing that can't you?

LA CALA Private Club. You've never dreamed of this. French with two mouths, four hands caressing your body. Dare yourself. Ring us. Visits. Striptease. 24 hours. 000000000

She would scare me to bloody death with 2 mouths and 4 hands.

MONICA twentysomething. CorDobesan model! (Fellatio without), 69 vibrators, Greek, very hot. Try. 000000000

69 vibrators—and there's that 'Greek' again!

CAN YOU IMAGINE SEEING THOSE IN YOUR LOCAL RAG?

THE FARMACIA (CHEMIST)

Things are no doubt different inland at the small towns and villages, but generally speaking, in the major resorts along the Costa del Sol the Farmacia's are brilliant. Most speak perfect English and almost act as a doctor. As with anything, some are better and friendlier than others but you can go into many of them, explain your problem, and they are more than willing to give you advice and prescribe the necessary drugs or medicines. Also, unlike the UK, you can get antibiotics straight over the counter. If you had a serious ailment then you would be well advised to go to a doctor or to the hospital but the Farmacia's are as good as many British GP's.

What about the prices of drugs and medicines? They are much cheaper than in the UK and in certain instances much much cheaper. How can that be when the UK has the National Health Service? I have been astonished on many occasions at how little certain medications cost and some tourists actually buy pharmaceuticals in bulk to take home.

THE VET

As with the Farmacia's, the vets here are great. I obviously cannot comment on many of them, but the ones we have used have been absolutely fantastic. They speak perfect English, are very helpful and don't rush you. People who move abroad and bring their pets with them worry about veterinary care just as much as they do about their own medical care – don't!

I have a serious phobia – hypodermic needles! You show me one of those and I'm gone. Less than a second and I am on the floor. I even passed out in the hospital when my son Oliver was born. I was okay with the actual birth but a nurse then proceeded to take a hypodermic needle towards my wife and that was it, gone! I woke up in the hospital corridor with my head between my legs and a nurse telling me to take deep breaths – what a tosser! We have taken Dino to the vets on numerous occasions for various reasons but during one visit the vet picked up a package which I knew was a needle. Wooooh, stop there, if you get that out now then I'm a gonner, as in, on your floor. 'No problem, just go outside and I will call you back in when I have finished' he said. Sure enough, a couple of minutes later the vet called me back in and sat me down. He proceeded to tell me that for many years he had a serious phobia with elevators and that he had sympathy with my situation. 'Have you had therapy,' he said. Well no but I'm not insane, I just don't like needles! He went over to the cabinet, took out two brand new hypodermic needles still in their packets, and gave them to me. 'That's a start' he said, 'when you feel that you can do it, open them and just handle them. That's all, it may help you.' How nice can you get, he didn't have to do that. Unfortunately I'm still shit scared of needles.

On top of all that, the Vets over here charge a fraction of what they do in the UK.

Spanish vets – great!

THE CARRETERA

This is the dual carriageway which runs along the coast of the Costa del Sol. It's a racetrack where there are no rules. This is pure Mad Max stuff, anything goes. Overtaking, undertaking, tailgating to the extent that some of them might as well sit on the back seat of the car in front.

Come to think of it they sometimes do, that's where they finish up. Bumps, pile ups, multiple shunts are all just a tale of everyday folk for users of the carretera. You think it's crazy on the M25, M1 or M62, that's tame. People go for gaps in a Merc here that you wouldn't dare go for in a Smart Car in the UK, it's a complete shambles. They built a beautiful new motorway about a kilometer inland to take volume traffic off the carretera but charge people for using it. Result – nobody uses it, it's empty. When I say its empty, I mean empty. There is no charge for the stretch from Malaga to Fuengirola and it is packed, but if you carry on after Fuengirola you think the world has ended and nobody has told you. You can drive for miles and not see another vehicle until you get to the first toll booth at Callahonda and have to wake the attendant up.

Chris and I were driving along the carretera one day when a car seemed to come up behind us from nowhere with its headlights on full. I thought it was the police at first. For some reason this car slowed down when it got level with me and then cut straight across the front of our car. I slammed on the brakes in order to avoid yet another bash on the front wing. This car then sauntered on in front and I noticed an 'L' plate in the rear window. He was a learner and presumably the guy teaching him had told the driver to slow down which he took too literally. THE 'L' PLATE WAS UPSIDE DOWN! Look at that, I said, he's a learner and the L plate is upside down. 'Oh yes' said Chris, 'but it will be the right way up further along the road when the car is on its roof.' Good answer, I never thought of that! To be fair when there is an accident on the carretera or anywhere else for that matter, the police have traffic moving in a fraction of the time that it would take in the UK. These guys don't mess about measuring tyre marks or listening to arguments about whose fault it was. Out comes the whistle, the Spanish police love their whistles, and an electric bright light baton. They will bounce a car out of the way if necessary but their first priority is to get that traffic moving again, and they do, quickly.

The carretera. Not for the faint hearted!

I FANCY A SPEED BOAT

If you live down here then at some point you will inevitably think to yourself, 'I fancy a speed boat.' You sit on the promenade or on the beach and see these things going past. You want one. In actual fact you can buy a second hand speed boat relatively cheaply, they are a similar price to a mid range car. Be careful! It is one thing buying a boat, but it is quite another thing getting it into the water. You cannot just drive down onto the beach and launch a boat at the waters edge, you require a birth in a harbour and that's expensive, in fact it's stupid. Chris's son, Jonathan, had a speed boat and moored it in Cabopino Port which is between Fuengirola and Marbella. During the summer months it cost him five hundred euros per month just to have it sat in the water, that's a small mortgage. He bought his speed boat and periodically went out in it. Get to the mouth of the harbour, 'shall I turn left or right,' drive/ride for a while, (I'm not sure whether you drive or ride a speed boat). It doesn't take long, 'I'm bored now,' take it back until next time. The novelty doesn't generally last very long and people sell them on within a few months. Sounds great – isn't!

THE THINGS YOU MISS

It is true to say that there is very little you cannot now buy along the Costa del Sol. The difference is that in the UK you can go into virtually any supermarket and get whatever you want in one hit. Over here you will know that one particular shop sells one product you are after, and then another will stock something else, so it can be a days job doing the shopping if you want specific British produce and brands. Different people like different things and some British people who live here are quite happy to settle for Spanish products in total without requiring anything else – but not many!

WHAT I MISS!

Our UK family, that goes without say. My mum Norma, my dad Frank, my son Oliver, Chris's daughter Justine and our UK grandchildren Billy and Sienna.

Gala pie – yum yum! For anyone who has never heard of gala pie, it is a large slab of pork pie with boiled eggs running through it. I would risk prison for a large slice of that with brown sauce on it.

Marzipan Fruits – more yum yums!

My best mate Norman. I miss him a lot (in a manly kind of way). Chris doesn't miss him as she thought he led me astray. Strange that. Norman's wife Jackie won't miss me as she thought it was me who led him astray!

My local pub, 'The Brown Horse' in Coley near Halifax. I love living here but there is hardly a Sunday lunchtime goes by when I don't think to myself, I wish I was there now, just for an hour.

The Karachi on Neil Street in Bradford, now that's a curry house. The guys knew me; I didn't even have to order. 'A meat and spinach Stuart?' Heaven!

Jokes – They are part of everyday office and shop floor life in the UK. Hardly a day used to go by without someone coming out with a new joke, sometimes good, sometimes bad, and sometimes a good joke seemed bad if the person telling it couldn't tell jokes properly. You don't get good jokes here.

Chris and I talk about this subject a lot and she misses different things to me. I asked her what would be the first things she would buy if she walked into a UK supermarket. 'A metal potato masher and a pair of oven gloves,' she said. Oh right, I can't say they are things I would have thought of. Okay Chris, what do you miss most about the UK? 'The spring lambs jumping around in the fields in Yorkshire.' I can't say that's something I would have thought of either.

The (things you miss) is often a topic of conversation in our local bar and the diversification of feedback is incredible. 'Being at Old Trafford on a Saturday afternoon. Some bastard's sat in my seat.' 'Thornton's chocolates.' 'Being indoors with fitted carpets and the central heating on full during a really cold winters day' – eh – are you mad, go back then!

CLING FILM – Why is it that the Spanish can't make proper cling film? Its film but it doesn't cling, it's crap. It's a plasi bag on a reel. Come on, a British manufacturer of (proper) cling film. There's a huge market out here in Spain just waiting for you. Everybody wants it. Pack it in a box printed with a huge Union Jack design on it and call it (**PROPER**) cling film. – Please!

When you can get the British brands you want, the chances are that you will pay through the nose for them. British hair care, shower and bath products are particularly expensive. When Chris visits the UK which is more often than me, she comes back with all sorts of things. She is happy to pay say £20 excess baggage as the saving she has made on Spanish prices 'if you can get them,' will be around £60 so it's well worth it.

Ooooh – Gala Pie!

THE THINGS I DON'T MISS

Traffic and long faces!

Before I left the UK I could do upwards of 50,000 miles a year. On a typical day I could get up in the morning and drive from near Halifax to Slough and back, or to Glasgow and back in the day and think nothing of it. For the last three years of my working life I commuted from near Halifax to Hinckley in Leicestershire, that's a 240 mile round trip. I loved the place and the people, but not that much. I was like a robot. When we do go back to the UK in order to visit family and friends, I am immediately gob smacked as soon as I drive our hire car out of the airport. Where are all these people going, where do they all live, is there enough room? You probably don't notice it as I certainly didn't when I lived there, but stand back from it for a while and take a look, it's lunacy. All day, every day.

Sundays, what's happened to Sundays? They were the quiet days when you washed the car, cut the grass – oh yes, and went to the pub at lunch time – great! Not now, I am sad when I am in the UK on a Sunday, it's not the same. The M62 seems to be just as busy on a Sunday as it is during the week and everybody seems to be queueing to get into one of those out of town shopping centres. People seem to feel that they have to go out and cheer themselves up by purchasing a new three piece suite which they don't really need, and probably can't afford. Don't start paying for a year, by which time the babies been sick on it, grandad has put fifteen cigarette burns in it, and it's completely shagged out. You haven't paid a penny off it yet, you're in debt!

Long face, walking with a stoop, and looking thoroughly pissed off. I was part of it, I was one of them, but I didn't notice. Whenever I go back to the UK everyone seems to be so bloody miserable. Before we moved to Spain, Chris's son used to say the same thing to us when he visited the UK. I found it quite offensive, what does he mean, I'm not miserable. I probably was to him! Over here most of the people we meet are holiday makers so I guess we see people at their best and therefore it is probably unfair to make a direct comparison. When you live in the UK, you just get on with things as you have always done but do me a favour, next time you are walking around town just take two minutes. Sit on a bench and observe the people walking past. They're pissed off, at least they look pissed off to me!

THE FURNITURE

We brought our own furniture over to Spain and I do not regret it one bit, it's one of the best things we did as if you are going to live in rented accommodation you do not want to live with rented accommodation furniture. Having said that, it has a short shelf life. Once you finally put your roots down and buy a place in Spain, you will find that the furniture which looked great in the UK does not usually go particularly well out here. It's down to personal taste at the end of the day, but if you were honest with yourself then you would probably agree that if you were buying a new lounge suite or a dining suite for your new home in Spain, then there is no way that you would choose the same ones you have brought with you. It has served a purpose in your rented accommodation and made you feel at home and comfortable. That's important, but it's now time for a change. Bring your own furniture but expect to sell it for a song or bin it once you decide to settle into your own Spanish home.

THE TRADITIONS

Now this is one thing I do admire above all about the Spanish people. Although they are part of the EEC there is none of this, 'we mustn't offend the minorities.' When they have a special day, they have a special day, and it's for them. If you want to watch, partake and be respectful of their day then that's fine, but it is (their day). They have so many saints days that us Brits lose count but they are proper events. There are the Ferria weeks, which are during different weeks in different towns but are important to the locals. There is a fair ground, the women dress in traditional Spanish costume and the little boys and girls will be dressed the same. They are proud of it and quite rightly so. There will be horse men, flamenco dancers, the full bit, and everyone will have a great time without getting completely legless.

Many towns, including Fuengirola, have an annual bull

run. Wooden shutters are erected at both sides of the road from the bull ring, around the block, and into a yard. I haven't measured it but this run is probably only about four hundred yards from start to finish. It only lasts a few minutes but hell, it's a laugh. Guys will be there in fancy dress with running trainers and dressed as bull fighters, Brits in shorts and flip flops (pissed up), trying to look brave. They wait for the doors to open and the **baby** bulls to run out along the bull run. If you saw one of these baby bulls coming towards you then I can guarantee that you would instantly fill your trousers (or shorts). They don't look much like babies close up and talk about run, they can out run a Ferrari. These guys who are laughing their tits off and trying to look hard, soon leg it over the wooden shutters and if they are not quite quick enough, then it's one up the jacksy. Forget about compensation. If you have any sense – just watch!

New Years Eve is also a great event in Spain. We went to the main Church square in Fuengirola for our first New Years Eve on the Costa del Sol. It was brilliant. The Council erected two stages and there were pop groups and Flamenco dancers at it all through the night. There is a tradition here that on the stroke of midnight you drink a glass of champagne and eat twelve grapes, one for each stroke of midnight. I had been forewarned of this so bought a bottle of bubbly and a bag of grapes. I took twenty four grapes, twelve for Chris and twelve for me. I hadn't thought this through properly as I had, without thinking about it, bought grapes with seeds in them. You try and eat one grape every second for twelve seconds when they have seeds in them. Having already had copious amounts of beer we were spitting and dribbling grape seeds and champagne all down our fronts looking like complete retards. The square was packed, you couldn't move, and there we are surrounded by Spaniards whilst spitting grape seeds all over the place. If you are ever in Spain whilst there is a Fiesta, go to it. You will not be disappointed and the local people will be delighted that you are interested.

GARDENS

I love gardening. I really really love gardening. I had a huge garden in the UK and spent every spare moment I could just pottering about. I could get home from work late, be really stressed, Chris would put a gin and tonic in my hand and I would wander about in MY garden. Ten minutes, I'm okay. I was by no means an expert gardener but I like to think that my garden was the best in the whole world. It was to me anyway. I feel as though I have had an arm amputated now. I walk out onto our balcony or up onto our roof terrace and there is no garden. The roof terrace is huge and is a kind of garden, but instead of grass I have ceramic tiles and terracotta pots. It's not the same. I'd look a bit of a knob head wandering round our roof terrace with a Hayter petrol mower! Our urbanization has beautiful communal gardens but they are not mine, sack the gardener, I'll do it for free. You can grow things in pots until hell freezes over but it's not the same. I have tried to create a little England and failed, many times. Spend a fortune on seeds, bulbs, compost, and what do you get – DEAD! Intense heat, salt from the sea air, you're shafted. ***Put up with the plants which were meant to be here – twigs!***

MAN SHOPPING

Believe it or not most men over here actually like shopping in supermarkets. Well, not the shopping bit, but going into the supermarket itself. Why? Because there is a bar – wheeeey – now that's shopping. You can visit virtually any major supermarket along the Costa del Sol and sure enough in the corner, there's a bar. Well it's actually a cafeteria, but it sells beer. You carry on love, here's a wedge of money, I'll just buy a newspaper and sit here for a while. I'll be okay – honest! An hour later and the lady returns to a half pissed husband who wants to stay in the shop a lot longer. 'What's changed from the UK, he hated shopping' – THEY SELL BEER!

LIFESTYLE GREAT (COMPLETELY DIFFERENT), BUT GREAT!

CHAPTER NINE

THAT'S IT – FOR NOW!

I really hope that you enjoyed reading my book as much as I enjoyed writing it. It is not a guide book; it isn't even a book of do's and don'ts. It is just something I felt I wanted to do in order to give people an insight into life on the Costa del Sol.

It doesn't take long to tell people what is good about southern Spain, its easy – sun, sea, sand – everyone already knows that!

When Chris read the finished article, she commented that she thought people may feel the book was a bit negative. I was actually quite pleased with that comment because it is important for the people who follow to know what they could be letting themselves in for. I have always enjoyed a good laugh but you can't laugh all of the time. When Chris and I came over here we didn't know anything about anything and not surprisingly, we fell foul of a few things. We have seen a number of sad cases where people didn't do their homework, didn't think things through, and their dream life in the sun turned into a horror film. Some disasters were caused through innocence and others were through sheer stupidity. You cannot move to Spain and permanently play at being on holiday unless you have a never ending supply of money which few people have. If you get it right, then you will never look back and you will wonder why you didn't do it years ago. If however, you get it wrong, then failure and disillusionment will be the order of the day.

If I could pick one statement out of this whole book to offer as advice, then it would be this one from chapter 3 –

'Just assume that everyone is out to rob you and you can then be pleasantly surprised when you find that they are not!'

Apart from that – Life really is a laugh on the Costa – honest!

One final point. You will remember that within this book I mentioned the fact that I had spent all of my UK working life in the printing industry. As such, I have had this book coated with a special intelligent varnish which makes the book self destruct if you lend it to anyone.

It explodes—honest! Tell them to buy their own bloody copy!

Adios!

ACKNOWLEDGEMENT

Thank you very much indeed to John Harrison. John read my original manuscript via The Literary Agency and was a tremendous help in terms of constructive criticism. I hope the final item is not a disappointment to him.

ISBN 1412086345

9 781412 086349